F

AFTER THE FIRE

THE DESTRUCTION OF THE
LANCASTER COUNTY
AMISH

◆

After the Fire

THE DESTRUCTION OF THE

LANCASTER COUNTY AMISH

◆

RANDY-MICHAEL TESTA

FOREWORD BY JOHN A. HOSTETLER

AFTERWORD BY ROBERT COLES

ILLUSTRATIONS BY

SUSIE RIEHL

◆

UNIVERSITY PRESS OF NEW ENGLAND   HANOVER AND LONDON

University Press of New England, Hanover, NH 03755
© 1992 by Randy-Michael Testa
All rights reserved
Printed in the United States of America 5 4 3 2 1
CIP data appear at the end of the book

The author acknowledges the following newspapers for permission to reprint articles: *The Lancaster Intelligencer Journal*, *The Lancaster Sunday News*, *The Sun Ledger*, *The Philadelphia Inquirer*, and *The London Sunday Independent*. The quote from Ignazio Silone's *Bread and Wine* (© 1937 by Harper & Bros.; © 1962 by Atheneum; English translation by Eric Mosbacher © 1986 by Darina Silone) is reprinted by permission of Russell and Volkening as agents for the author.

Some events have been altered to protect the identities
of certain individuals. Additionally,
Amish names have been
changed.

Elijah was afraid and fled for his life . . . and went a day's journey
into the desert, until he came to a broom tree and sat beneath
it. He prayed for death: "This is enough, O Lord! Take
my life, for I am no better than my fathers. . . ."

Then the Lord said, "Go outside and stand on the mountain before the
Lord; the Lord will be passing by." A strong and heavy wind was
rending the mountains and crushing rocks before the Lord—but
the Lord was not in the wind. After the wind there was an
earthquake—but the Lord was not in the earthquake.
After the earthquake there was a fire—but the
Lord was not in the fire. After the fire there
was a tiny whispering sound. When he
heard this, Elijah hid his face in
his cloak and went and stood
at the entrance to the
cave. —1 Kings
19:3–4; 11–13.

◆

FOREWORD

BY JOHN A. HOSTETLER

◆

For three centuries Lancaster County, Pennsylvania, has been a unique place because of its cultural and religious inheritance. It was here, in the heart of William Penn's woods, that the concept of religious freedom in the United States flowered. Unlike New England, where religious nonconformists were suspected of being witches and suffered harassment and death, in Penn's colony most of the inhabitants exercised restraint, moderation, and a sense of care about each other. The Amish and other "plain people" had responded to Penn's invitation to oppressed peoples to come to a place where they could live and worship freely.

Will the "plain" communities disappear from Lancaster County and from the face of the earth, as have numerous other holistic and intensely human communities? The forces of change and the pressures for "modernization" are descending upon the family, school, and community. The traditions and institutions of the past—in village, clan, tribe, and region—are greatly weakened or destroyed. The centralized bureaucratic state, urbanization, and mass communication have caused havoc with the social well-being of human beings. Mainstream society is marked by homelessness. There is widespread longing for community life.

The Old Order Amish, by way of contrast, have sought protection from the dangers of alienation. They have survived in modern times as small, viable, and distinctive communities, resisting modernization more successfully than many other ethnic and religious communities. Because they have moderated the influences of industrialization on their personal lives, their families, and their communities, they have not yet disappeared. They have quietly developed a community that is integrated with their values and a school system that does not produce alienated youths but rather dedicated adults. They stand out as meticulous farmers, practicing the virtues of thrift and hard work, and as islands of sanity in a society gripped by greed and technology run rampant.

◆

A few years ago, a young man who had completed all requirements for a doctoral degree except his dissertation wrote to me with a modest request. "Would it be possible to observe Amish children in their schools? I want to write about explicit education in a belief system—a faith community."

Of the many inquiries about the Amish I have received through the years, this one was the most difficult to lay aside. The writer informed me that he had taught third-grade children for five years. He wrote: "I am a Catholic, whose studies at Harvard have often found me spending more time in the Divinity School than in the School of Education. I have been teaching for Professor Cox's course 'Jesus and the Moral Life.' For two years I have taught for another man of faith in his own way—Robert Coles. He teaches a course titled 'The Literature of Social Reflection.' All of this led me to look long and hard at the idea of a community of faith—what it is and how it sustains itself."

The writer of these lines was Randy-Michael Testa.

Should I lend him encouragement? So many of those who seek to meet the Amish are caught up in personal searches for fulfillment. But I knew that any young man who had taught third grade for five years would not likely be inclined toward utopianism.

Randy recalled his one brief contact with the Amish: "Several years ago I had an encounter with an Amish family that was akin to being struck by lightning on a horse. I went for a five-mile run. At the crest of the hill I saw a wagon behind which was literally a mile's worth of traffic. An Amish family was moving to join their relatives in another state. I ran alongside of them for over a mile and a half, talking with them, keeping people from taking their pictures, steering cars around them, etc. I was moved by the encounter, by their faith, by their integrity—and by how kind they were to me."

He persisted in his request: "I hope you will consent to help me. What's in it for you? I cannot say, except that I can tell you, I'm a good student and absolutely earnest about my studies and their integrity as concerns the Amish."

The outcome of our subsequent discussions together, and of Randy's continuing association with the Amish community, is embodied in this book.

This is not "just another book." The marketplace is glutted with books and pamphlets on just about every aspect of Amish life. The reader of this volume will not be confronted with claims of new sociological insights, analytical research findings, or theological discourse. The knowledge contained in this book does not derive from what can be measured statistically or tested in a laboratory. Instead, this book advances the method of personal narrative and human awareness. It is readable, inviting, believable, and enlightening. It communicates what moral life in a faith community is all about.

The ethical questions raised in this volume will cut to the heart. It will make the greedy uncomfortable and humiliate the pious.

Lancaster County has been a special place. In the midst of it, a faith community is struggling for survival. At stake is a national treasure. Two ways of life are competing for fulfillment. The one is maximizing material prosperity, comforts, protection, and status. The other way looks upon the maximization of material prosperity as a disease, deeply destructive of the way humankind was intended to live.

ACKNOWLEDGMENTS

◆

I would like to thank Pennsylvania friends Linda Coho and Hank Kline for tireless hospitality and kindness; Dick and Penny Armstrong for courage; Shirley Wenger of the Double Heart Gallery in Intercourse and Susie Riehl for their belief in this journey; Paul Alpaugh in Governor Casey's office for listening; the reporters of the Lancaster newspapers for keeping their eyes and ears open; and my parents, for the use of the Horizon.

I thank Wendell Berry for his wisdom.

I thank Robert Coles for his abiding example.

I thank Carol Gilligan for the courage to listen to the tiny whispering voice.

I thank Richard Haney-Jardine, a goad and a good friend.

I thank my editor, Mike Lowenthal, whom I first met at a barnraising in Goshen, Pennsylvania. The improbability of a man from Dartmouth and a man from Harvard convening among the Amish confirms my belief in grace.

I thank Sara Lawrence Lightfoot for the fellowship that made possible my initial trek to Pennsylvania.

I thank Hugh Silk for his help with a thousand things.

I thank the "Stoltzfus" family of Lancaster County, Pennsylvania. Through example, faith, large-heartedness and love, they taught me what St. Theresa calls "the little way." Rare is the person who can claim to have a second family. I have been so blessed.

This book is dedicated to John Hostetler, a lone prophet crying out in the moral wilderness of Pennsylvania. John made this entire journey possible. Thank you, John.

Finally, I thank God—for putting something so quiet and powerful in my road that day. I ask: how can one family's exodus from precariousness become another man's journey into grace? Are the two roads one? The answer is not for understanding. It is for believing. Now that these stories are told, I pray to believe them untrue.

INTRODUCTION

◆

The Amish stop people dead in their tracks. They are living question marks, confounding witnesses. People must either answer the questions posed by an Amish presence, or put the Amish out of sight so their witness will not shame secular souls.

In the summer of 1988, I lived and worked with an Amish family in Lancaster County, Pennsylvania. Since that time I have been back there at least once a month. This is the story of what I have witnessed in Pennsylvania.

Rampant development of farmland and a changing economy are turning Lancaster County into a bedroom suburb for Philadelphia, Baltimore, and Harrisburg. Meanwhile, the Amish population of Lancaster County continues to grow, while tourists from everywhere come to gawk.

After reading a much earlier draft of this manuscript, an Amish woman I know who makes quilts wrote:

Thank you for sharing a part of you, a chapter of your life. It's good. I was moved—deeply. Actually, it almost makes me want to be Amish . . . .

My critique is this: you painted the "English" too bad and the Amish too good. "There is some good in the worst of us and there is some bad in the best of us." The Amish world is not a Utopia. We are not saints. Maybe *I* should write a book. I could tell stories of family feuds, swindlings, wife beaters, child molesters, incest, and suicide, the whole gamut. True, these are not the norm, but are they in the "outside world"?

Life doesn't come in black and white but subtle shades and hues of gray.

But I see that for the story you are telling it helps to darken the darks and lighten the lights for contrast.

With this critique in mind, I reworked the book into its present form. I wrote back to my friend saying I did not wish to idealize or denigrate either group, but that I hoped the book would be like another Amish friend says about his stubborn mules, "Sometimes to get them to do anything you practically have to whack them with a plank." Or, in the words of Flannery O'Connor: "When you can assume that your audience holds the same beliefs you do, you can relax a little and use more normal means of talking to it; when you have to assume that it does not, then you have to make your vision apparent by shock—to the hard of hearing you shout, and for the almost-blind you draw large and startling figures."

Writing about two conflicting worlds is tricky, and all the more so when one group chooses not to speak for itself. *I cannot and do not claim to speak for the Amish.* I claim only to say what I know from living briefly in their world, and in reflecting on life in my own.

I have attempted to dramatize the spiritual relationship between two very different worlds: the Old Order Amish of Lancaster County, Pennsylvania, and the surrounding society that threatens to drive them out of an area long known as "the Garden Spot of America." This is a painful story for me to tell, but an infinitely more painful story for those living it. I feel I must tell it—must "whack the reader with a plank"—because the Amish will not do it themselves. Their religion enjoins them to be a nonresistant people who remain apart from the "affairs of men."

In places I risk sermonizing in the expression of my opinions (which unless otherwise stated, are entirely my own). At other times I am quarrelsome in tone. For all this I apologize in advance, offering as explanation Dorothy Day's words: "If I sound preachy or didactic, it is because I am preaching and teaching myself on this narrow road we are all traveling."

Amish society turns three hundred years old in 1993. As of this writing, it remains to be seen what that anniversary will portend. Can the Amish remain in Lancaster County? As I see it, this is the story of a people on the verge of conflagration.

AFTER THE FIRE

THE DESTRUCTION OF THE
LANCASTER COUNTY
AMISH

◆

PART ONE

As he looked down toward . . . the whole region . . . he
saw dense smoke over the land rising like fumes
from a furnace. —Genesis 19:28

◆

It was the summer of the film *Witness*.

After five years of teaching third grade at a private school in Denver, I was spent. I had nothing left for anyone. I was tired, morally
tired. I had taught over 120 children how to multiply up to nine, to
read paperback accounts of flying saucers and the Loch Ness mon-
ster, and to sing "O Tannenbaum" on squeaky wooden risers in a
drafty gymnasium for the annual, all-school Christmas pageant.

I had been wined and dined by parents who owned the Rio Grande
Railroad and most of the banks on skyscraper-darkened Seven-
teenth Street in Denver; by parents who sat on the boards of the
Symphony, the Zoo, and the Museum of Natural History—all of
whose children were somehow in my charge.

These same parents had frequently asked me over for dinner and
I went gladly, tooling from house to house on a banana-yellow moped
with a briefcase full of phonics sheets strapped onto the back with
a bungee cord. At dinner the talk was as rich as the gourmet food
served. It was a great comfort at first to find one's self the member
of an inviting, prosperous community—accounted for, in a sense.
Parents shared their concerns and afforded their hospitality—tacit
demonstrations of gratitude in the private school world.

Yet behind the pleasant family facades, the world of privileged,

1

upper-crust Denver had begun to crumble. In the late 1970s and early '80s, the city was in the middle of an oil boom. Developers went crazy, building development after development from downtown Denver all the way down the Front Range to Colorado Springs. The oil brought up from deep in the earth fired the city's craving for excess.

Businessmen paid cash for million-dollar estates. One man bought his wife a lime-green Cadillac with license plates that read "A PRESENT." When the youngest daughter of one family turned sixteen, her family rented out the Brown Palace Hotel. Dozens of caged wild animals from Africa were trucked into the lobby, and the theme of the evening was "Safari Night." People walked amidst the wild animals in their best clothing eating scallops wrapped in bacon atop little pieces of bread with the crusts trimmed away.

But after a few years the Western oil became more expensive to bring up than it was worth, and the boom went bust. People had been living far beyond their means, moving too quickly into what was not theirs. "For Sale" signs sprouted around the Country Club like mushrooms; moving vans criss-crossed the neighborhood. Now, like the oil fields that had dotted its surroundings, the Denver of ease and money was dry: economically, morally, spiritually.

As the city's fashionable base crumbled, so did the lives of those who had relied on too much money too fast. In my last year of teaching, more than half my students were seeing psychiatrists—because their parents could not or would not "parent." I went to dinner at the home of a child who soiled his pants regularly on the playground because he was convinced his father was going to kill him. At the table there was pleasant conversation, good food, luscious red wine. Suddenly, as the father leaned on the rim of his wine glass with the palm of his opened hand, the glass stem snapped. The top of the glass tipped over and the cracked stem shot through his palm. There was blood. The father said with curious detachment as he wrapped his hand in a linen napkin, "Gee, I didn't know I was hanging on that hard."

Three school fathers committed suicide in as many years: one, unable to contain his alcoholism, in a closed garage with the engine of his ancient, maroon BMW; a second, facing the fact that the oil

2

wells he bought were now dry, with a shotgun blast to his left temple; a third, upon learning of terminal illness, by locking the bathroom door and shooting himself through the heart with a pistol while his wife and children ate pizza in the next room.

How could the children of such parents know what to do with the darkness they beheld? How could *I*? I am not a priest, I reminded parents—and myself. I am not a psychiatrist, I am a teacher. Every day I wondered what it meant to hand a child worksheets knowing that a custody battle was raging out of control at home.

I applied for and was accepted into the doctoral program at Harvard's Graduate School of Education, to specialize in moral education. I left Denver and went to my parents' home near Valley Forge National Park in Pennsylvania. I left Denver, not because I was "looking for something"; I left because I had seen enough.

I spent the summer with my mother and father—sitting in the bleachers at Phillies games with my dad, going to outlet stores in Reading to buy new boxer shorts, an ironing board, and pots and pans with my mother. It was mundane and relaxing.

But at night I had a recurring dream: the school was ablaze. Covered in soot and ash, I dragged half-dead children out of the flames while the other teachers sat in their classrooms, moving in slow motion. The oddest part about this dream was that in the middle of the flames, my heart would stop beating. I awakened each night with a jolt.

Running through the green expanses and rolling hills of nearby Valley Forge National Park helped quench the orange fires blazing out of control in the center of my dreams. I ran until I stopped hearing the screams of children covered with the soot of parental indifference. I ran and ran and ran. I ran until once again I could hear my own heart beating.

PART TWO

They had been rushed out of Egypt and had no
opportunity even to prepare food for the
journey. —Exodus 12:39

◆

I was running along the trails of Valley Forge National Park when I saw it: a covered wagon traveling down Route 23. Not some "living history" display manned by cynical undergraduates in colonial costumes with sneakers underneath, but a real Conestoga wagon. Pots and pans dangled from its sides. A collie and two little girls looked out from the wobbly canvas cover.

I ran up to the driver's side. "Hello! Where are you folks heading?" I asked, panting to keep up.

The people inside peered out warily. I was startled. They were Amish.

The father wore a sky-blue short-sleeved shirt, wide-brimmed straw hat, and black suspendered pants. His eyes were gray. The mother wore a simple navy dress and a white cap. Her hands were clenching the sides of the wagon. Both parents were barefoot.

The girls climbed up to the front of the wagon. The collie came forward too. It was panting and the spit coating its tongue looked like soap suds.

"What are you doing on Route 23 in the middle of the summer?" I asked. "This is tourist season!"

Striped yellow campers, automobiles with bicycles strapped to their trunks, and tour buses full of senior citizens crawled behind us. Traffic was rapidly backing up.

5

"Oh, tourists," the mother said, then she said something to her husband in Pennsylvania Dutch. They both laughed nervously, and regarded me wearing a Walkman and running shorts as if to say, "And you? What might you be?"

"We thought Route 23 would be the best way to get to Philadelphia for our way of traveling," the father said. They had already covered forty miles, he added.

"Where are you heading, traveling like this?"

"For a new settlement of our people in Tennessee."

The horses' sides were heaving like accordion bellows; their bodies were stained with brown-smelling sweat under the reins. One horse frothed at the mouth. It was 94 degrees. As can only happen during moments of complete disorientation, it suddenly occurred to me: the horses might die in this heat.

Tourists began jumping out of their slowing cars to take pictures. "Hey, Aay-mish! Look, Aay-mish people!" they shouted. A bald man in blue plastic thongs and a "Pennsylvania Dutch Country" T-shirt stuck his hand in front of one of the horses, and it jerked with a start.

The mother said something in an undertone to the father in "Dutch." The father squinted. I watched his gray eyes, watched as they searched for anything even faintly recognizable in this worldly morass—a farm, a produce stand—watched them narrow as he must have wondered if he would ever again be within the protective confines of an Amish community. I thought of the Psalm: "How shall we sing the Lord's song in a strange land?"

"Do you know where we might pull out of this traffic and water our horses?" the father suddenly asked.

"Follow me," I said. I felt a protective surge well up.

Suddenly, a blond man about my age in a fire-engine red spandex cycling outfit appeared alongside the covered wagon riding an expensive yellow bicycle. In one smooth, uninterrupted motion the cyclist pulled out a camera with an enormous lens and aimed it into the Amishman's face.

Something inside me snapped. The camera became a gun, the man preparing to shoot it, some sort of carbetbagger. I was confused by these thoughts and the intensity of my feelings. In a split second

I felt as if I had been yanked from my own world, made a stranger to it. I was ashamed of it, both a part of it and apart from it, enraged by it, sickened by it as suddenly as I had been when watching a glass stem snap and then shoot through a father's hand.

I looked at the Amish father. His eyes had narrowed again. "Forgive me," I said to him quietly.

I wanted to put a stick into the spokes of the cyclist's rear wheel, wanted to watch him fly off the embankment and go skipping like a stone across the wide, mowed fields of the park. Instead I put my hand over the camera lens and shouted, "PUT THAT STUPID THING AWAY AND GET OUT OF HERE, YOU SELFISH MORON!"

The cyclist veered away from the wagon, and the wheels of his bicycle hummed as he flew down Route 23.

I led the covered wagon off the road, down a running trail to a Ranger station. Two tall rangers in green shirts and khaki pants were sitting at a picnic table under a tree. They were passing a pack of Camel filters back and forth. Their hats were on the ground. At the sight of a man in running shorts leading a covered wagon crowded with Amish people pulled by four massive, gray Percherons, the rangers jumped to their feet, doused their cigarettes in the nearby horse trough, and put their hats back on.

"Well!" said the first ranger, pushing his hat back and scratching his head. "You folks sure are a long way from home. Let's water the horses; they look like they're not doing so well. These are beautiful Percherons."

"Thank you," the father said.

The rangers took the reins from the Amishman and led his horses to the trough. The horses drank in long, low, even slurps. When they finished, the horses shook their heads back and forth slowly, working to readjust the bits in their mouths with a chomping metal sound. The mother took a scratched black skillet from the side of the wagon, filled it with brackish trough water, and set it on the ground. The collie drank with a lapping rhythm and the girls climbed out of the wagon to watch. In fact, we all stood watching the dog drink—transfixed.

I looked at the girls. Both were barefoot. Their hair was plaited, parted down the middle in severe, straight, beautiful parts. They

7

wore simple green dresses. The younger of the two looked at the dog and then at the rangers and explained, "He's thirsty."

"We're much obliged," the father said to the first ranger. The second went inside a maintenance shed about thirty feet down the trail. He came back a minute later with a large burlap bag full of oats. "It's not a lot, but I think it oughta help," he said.

"Well! Thank you!" the father said. "What's our bill?" I could feel him relax among this group of "English." The dulling squint was gone. The rest of the family got back into the wagon.

"No charge," the second ranger said. "I was born in Lancaster County. We had Amish neighbors."

Stunned silence.

Then, "OH! I *see!*" The Amish woman looked at her husband. It was as if the ranger had said the secret password.

"I don't suppose you've got some shoo-fly pie back in there somewhere?" the ranger asked, sensing the change and winking at the girls. They smiled back.

"No! Imagine! I didn't do any baking for this trip! We hurried to finish packing. I knew I should've brought some along. Why, I should be ashamed!" the mother said, her eyes flashing.

"How about *you* folks? Anything you need?" asked the first ranger.

"Maybe a prayer," the father said quietly. There was a pause.

"If I give you my address, will you write and let me know you arrived safely?" I asked.

"Surely we can," the father said. One of the girls took out a little book and a pencil. I wrote my name and address with the thick pencil, teethmarks gouged into its tip.

The father looked at my name. "Ran-dy Tes-ta. Where are your people from?" he asked.

"My father's father was born in Sicily," I said.

"I see. . . . Well. Guess we better be off. We're hoping to be past Philadelphia tonight," he said. "Thank you again." He urged the horses on. And then they pulled away.

I shook hands with both rangers and ran behind the covered wagon as it turned out onto Route 23—back into summer traffic—until it reached the edge of the park, headed for a screaming expressway ramp. The girls waved from the back.

Then the father turned around suddenly, leaning out far to the right on the wooden seat. He put his left hand into the air. "Thank you, stranger!" he shouted over the wooden rumble of wagon wheels. Then they were engulfed by traffic.

I looked hard. The vision was gone. The covered wagon had vanished. I stood for a minute. I could see heat rising from the expressway. I ran back and stood at the entrance to the park—the place where the wagon first appeared. I sat down under a tree, hid my face in my hands, and wept.

PART THREE

The angel of the Lord encampeth round them
that fear Him, and delivereth
them. —Psalm 34:7

◆

May 21, 1988. Phoenixville, Chester County, PA.

I awake at 5:45 A.M., wandering around my parents' house in a fog. By seven I am sitting behind the maroon steering wheel of the green Plymouth Horizon they are lending me for the summer. I travel down Route 30 bound for Paradise, Lancaster County. I am heading toward something I do not even know how to think about.

◆

It was hazy and humid, a close but cold morning as it can be only in Pennsylvania, lacking for any hint of a breeze. On the seat next to me was a splayed map of Lancaster County. I was traveling down Route 30 carrying two suitcases of clothing, a Bible, a copy of *David Copperfield*, a ream of typing paper, a Westclox key-wound alarm clock ticking away on the dashboard, and a black 1908 Underwood typewriter. I wondered when and where I should turn off. Every now and then I glanced at the map, as if looking at it would reveal what the summer among the Amish would portend. I listened as Handel faded in and out of the Philadelphia public radio station, becoming scratchier and scratchier the further on I drove.

Turning off Route 30 in Lancaster County, I made my way to Harvest Drive, toward an 'X' on the map that would be the farm of an Amishman named Elam J. Stoltzfus.

Just outside the business district of Intercourse, the Horizon coasted to a standstill. I tried turning the ignition key several times. Nothing. I tried again. Nothing. The ENGINE light's orange glow came on and the pointy click of the key twisted impotently. I said, "Oh Jesus," and put my head against the steering wheel.

A herd of black and white Holsteins stood bawling indignantly at the edge of the field near the Horizon. I was at a complete loss as to what to do next. I got out of the car and looked at it. It was surrounded by pasture. I noticed the house across the road and its mailbox, which read CHRIST B. ZOOK. Three little Amish children were spying on me from behind drawn, green blinds.

Several pickup trucks whizzed by. I tried the key again because it is the only thing I know how to do with a car. Two gray-topped Amish carriages went by. The drivers waved their Amish wave, moving one hand in a slight arc while holding onto the reins. I sat down on the hood of the Horizon thinking that in Boston no one would stop for a stranded motorist so why would this place be any different?

It was very, very quiet. I heard steam hissing from under the Horizon's hood and my alarm clock ticking away on the dashboard.

At that very moment a thundering black truck stopped. Daniel Esh offered me a lift. In his mid-sixties, a "Beachy" Amishman (I would find out later that this means, among other things, that he trims his beard, owns and drives a car, and uses electricity), Esh told me he'd just come from a Saturday-morning prayer meeting. We pushed the car off Harvest Drive into the pasture where by now cows bawled so furiously that I envisioned them storming the fence.

"Where are you trying to go?" Esh asked.

"To Elam Stoltzfus's farm—on Belmont Road."

There was a pause. "Elam Stoltzfus?" he asked with the characteristic Pennsylvania intonation that goes up mid-sentence. "Do you know him?"

I told Esh about helping Elam while I also "do some writing for school."

I avoided the words "thesis" and "dissertation." I avoided telling my rescuer about sociologist John Hostetler and his assistance

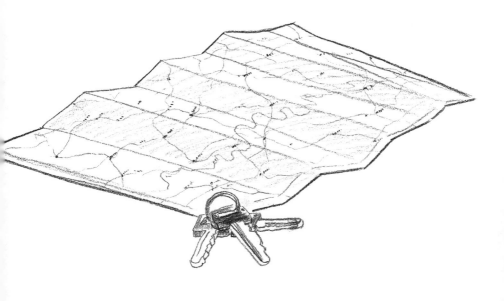

in finding a place for me to live and work in Lancaster County in response to a letter I had written in April. I avoided saying I had come from Harvard to "obtain data" about a "moral community" so that I could "write up" my "field notes" gleaned from the stance of "participant-observer." Instead I sat with my hands folded in my lap.

While we drove down Belmont Road, Daniel Esh turned to me suddenly. "Are you a Christian?" he asked.

"Yes, a Catholic," I replied.

Esh glanced sideways over at me, a look that said in another time his people, the Amish, were tortured and killed by Catholics—my people.

Thinking again of what might be happening if this were Boston, I said, "I sure hope the farmer who owns that land won't mind having a broken-down Horizon pushed onto it."

"Won't mind at all," Esh said, "I own it."

We drove through farmland unlike any I had seen: groomed and ordered, fields like green sketches of symmetry, neat white barns, tobacco sheds and farmhouses. But for lolling cows, there were few signs of life about—just an occasional wash line, the sound of an engine running from a lane off Belmont Road, a lone Amishman on a push-scooter going down the hill, his right foot propelling him with wide, one-legged strides. At the bottom of a hill just before a little creek there was a large red mailbox shaped like a barn. It read ELAM STOLTZFUS. Daniel Esh gave me his card so I would be able to tell the Stoltzfuses where my car had broken down. Under his name there was a line from Scripture: "The angel of the Lord encampeth round them that fear Him, and delivereth them."—Psalm 34:7.

And then Daniel Esh screeched away like a high school boy late for a dance.

◆

I stand looking at the large white farmhouse, stately as it sits facing the creek that winds through the meadow in front of it. White ducks rest on the creek's banks. Porch chimes tinkle distractedly.

Rachel Stoltzfus comes out the front door and stands with her fists on her hips. At sixty-five, she is stout, about 5′ 5″ tall, with a round face and quick gray-blue eyes. Her gaze is so penetrating I feel I

14

am standing naked in the driveway. She is wearing a black dress, Amish style, pinned with straight pins in the back, a white cap over her gray hair with two white ribbons at either side, half tied together at the top of her chest, and wire spectacles.

"Hello, Mrs. Stoltzfus," I stammer red-faced, "I know this is a heck of a way to begin but my car is broken down a couple of miles from here on the land of the man who just dropped me off his name is—" and I fumble for the card in my pocket—"His name is Daniel Esh."

A pause while I am sized up head to toe. "Well, come on in and talk to Elam," Rachel Stoltzfus says, while a black Chihuahua named Shorty yips incessantly the minute I place a foot on the wooden, green-painted porch steps.

"He'll warm up to you after a while. Call me Rachel."

I feel like running after Daniel Esh's truck.

Rachel fetches her husband from a side room on the first floor where he has been sleeping. I try not to stare or look around. Elam Stoltzfus appears, sleepy-headed, without spectacles, his long white beard and hair tousled.

"Well, hello! You made it!" he says, yawning.

I tell him about the Horizon in the midst of the Holsteins. Instantly Elam and Rachel start speaking animated Dutch.

This is quite a moment for all of us, it seems.

After a moment, Rachel says, "Our son Levi will drive you back to your car and help you get your things."

Rachel walks through a high-shelved room full of black leatherbound books and a SCANDIA brand gravity-inversion machine—essentially a cot that swings straight upward vertically on a metal stand, causing the person reclining on it to be supported by the ankles while standing on his or her head.

The sight of this contraption for lower back pain throws me. Rachel opens a door of the study leading to a bedroom, and then opens another door that leads to a sparse kitchen. She and Elam live in the "doddy haus," (the "grandfather house") now that their youngest son, Levi, is married and has his own family. Levi, twenty-six, lives in the part of the house in which Elam and Rachel raised their five daughters and five sons, now with *his* wife, Katie, twenty-five,

15

and their three children—Rebecca, four, Benuel, two, and Samuel, five months.

Levi Stoltzfus follows his mother back to where Elam and I are standing in her kitchen. He is tall for an Amishman—about 6′ 2″—and his beard is dark brown and thickly tufted. Levi wears a black coat, black pants and black suspenders, knee-length rubber boots, slightly tinted rectangular wire-rimmed spectacles, and a wide-brimmed black felt hat. He looks like an Amish mountain man. We are introduced, shake hands, and my little hand completely disappears into his. Like his father's beard, Levi's is trimmed to the outline of his face; there is no mustache, it simply grows long and scraggly from under his chin.

"I can take you to your car," he says.

"I know this is a heck of a way to begin, but all I can say is I'm sorry," I offer to Levi, Elam, and Rachel. And off Levi and I walk to the barn.

Levi fetches a chestnut-colored mare named Pat from the horse stalls and begins to hitch her up. "So," he asks offhandedly, "do you have any experience with barn animals?"

"No."

"Well, the thing to remember is that when you approach a horse, don't surprise him."

It is now 9:20 A.M. Levi, his little moon-faced son, Benuel (who is barefoot, runny-nosed, and wearing a black, bonnetlike hat, black pants, and a black coat), Rebecca (in a royal blue woolen scarf and sky blue cotton dress), and I (in culture shock) drive to Harvest Drive in Levi and Katie's spindly black carriage with its gray vinyl top. Levi points out the green and brown stripes of land he works.

"Corn and hay's what we grow; it's what's most profitable for us right now."

Benuel and Rebecca have their heads stuck out the back window of the carriage the entire way, just above where the luminous orange safety triangle hangs on the back of what is called a "market wagon."

Clip-clip, clip-clip, clip-clip, clip-clip, clip-clip, clip-clip, clip-clip, clip-clip, clip-clip, clip-clip, clip-clip is the rhythm here: horse hooves on asphalt road moving at twelve miles an hour. It gets inside you, changes your expectations; it lets you look into the faces of cows

16

as you pass, lets you see their eyelashes. Benuel is humming. The world is new.

I have been here less than two hours. I am forty miles away from my mother and father across a galaxy of custom and sensibility where nothing I know is apt or fitting. I have indeed been delivered—to a place where everything is new and it is the first day of a school where books and theory simply collapse in the face of Levi Stoltzfus smoking his pipe behind Pat's steady gait as we pass his seventy acres of immaculate land on a cold damp morning in May.

◆

Levi listens to the engine as I turn the key. "Sounds to me like you broke a belt, but I can't say for sure."

"You're not even allowed to drive these things and you know more about a car than I do," I say.

"Well, an engine is an engine," he replies.

Rebecca and Benuel have gotten out of the buggy. Rebecca picks a thin, bright buttercup and gives it to Benuel, who then carefully places it in the hood of the car. Levi strides right out to the middle of Harvest Drive and flags down the first truck that comes by. The big man in its cab, wearing a red baseball cap says, "Yep?"

"Can we call on you for help?" Levi says.

"Depends on what it is."

"Would you know the best garage we could take this car to— a place where they would really be able to fix this engine for a fair price?"

The man in the truck relaxes. "Sure, what's wrong with it?"

"It won't start," I say lamely. "The thing that says ENGINE goes on but the car won't roll over."

The man in the red hat calls a garage from the phone in his truck. As he is doing so, he asks, "What year car is it?"

"It's a 1979—I think."

The man gets out of his cab. He hunches over the Horizon, lifts the hood and scratches away some caked oil from under the hood. "See these numbers right here?" he says looking up at me. "These're what you need when you go to the garage. Write them down." He

17

goes back to the truck. After a moment he says, "The garage I called don't have Horizon parts."

"Well, thank you kindly for your time," Levi says.

"No trouble at all," he says, zooming away.

My heart lightens as the sun burns away the fog and the cold. We pull into a cinder-block garage. A crooked, hand-lettered sign plastered on the door with masking tape reads "MAY 21st ONLY WE WILL OPEN AT 11 A.M." Levi and I look at each other. It is 9:40 and I start laughing, at my timing, at the goofy sign, at the fact that I have no idea minute by minute what will happen next in this place. And Levi starts laughing at me and says, "Well, let's try another place."

We drive into Intercourse, toward a Getty's station in the heart of the village. Pulling into the gas station, Levi says, "Maybe you can see what they'll do for you."

I jump out of the buggy. I quietly explain my circumstances to the man whose shirt pocket says MARTIN. He checks with his boss to see if they can tow the car in. I run to Levi. "I think this is going to work," I tell him. "I'm very grateful to you, Levi."

"I hope they can fix it for you," he says, and with a jerk on the reins, Levi, Benuel, and Rebecca drive away. Martin and I drive back to the Horizon in his red truck. He brings some electrical testing equipment with which to test the ignition wires. En route, he tells a story. "After my father died, mother and I got $5,800 per acre for the farm. We sold all the hogs too because the farm was $150,000 in debt. But we made enough on the sale to pay all the bills and build Mom a little house. We sold the farm to a developer. They're building houses on it now." Then he is silent.

Would I do for these people what they have done for me if this were Harvard Square? No. But here. Here, I would do more, I tell myself.

I think so.

At the car Martin pokes around with his tools and flashlight for a few minutes, his head disappearing under the hood. He re-emerges saying, "The belt's snapped. See here? We'll have to tow it to the shop."

While I wait for the Horizon to be repaired, I sit on the curb

18

in front of the Getty's service station at the intersection of Routes 772 and 340 in the center of Intercourse. On this Saturday morning, the Amish move swiftly in and out of Intercourse, bustling from the Dauphin Deposit Bank to Zimmerman's Dry Goods Store. By eleven o'clock, Amish market wagons give way to a steady, day-long stream of tourist congestion—vans and campers from Virginia, station wagons from New Jersey, caravans of tour buses from everywhere, and motorcycles carrying senior citizens.

Tourists in pastels and shorts troop by in throngs. In front of a store called BRASS WORLD, an exasperated father in a baseball cap, boots, blue jeans, and a huge silver belt buckle stiffens his arm, winds it straight back like a baseball player, then whacks his whining son on the seat so hard that the boy flies ten feet forward on the sidewalk. Walking behind, the wife and two little daughters look hot and wilted. Busloads of elderly people pull into the gigantic parking lot of KITCHEN KETTLE VILLAGE, a conglomeration of tourist shops selling jelly, Amish clothes for Cabbage Patch dolls, and T-shirts with slogans like: "Virginia May Be for Lovers but Pennsylvania Has Intercourse."

Weaving in and out of all the congestion—and the inadvertent reason for it—are the last of the Amish in their buggies: first, two adolescent boys in a rig loaded with spoked wheels, and then a mother with her two young children driving in an open cart as confidently as a suburban mother in her Volvo station wagon, taking a turn at carpool.

Suddenly, as if at a signal, the Amish vanish.

A woman turns to her husband as he eats an ice cream cone. "We haven't seen one Aay-mish yet," she complains. "Where are they?"

The Amish are at home, on their farms, and in their shops, hidden away from the scramble overtaking Intercourse and Routes 30 and 340. They have ducked out of the limelight in order to go about their lives.

And the sight of so much frenetic activity as I sit waiting on the curb at the Getty's station is comic and terrible, both.

PART FOUR

When the day of Pentecost came it found them
gathered in one place. —Acts 2:1

◆

*It is eighteen years ago that Anette Scherer, a then twenty-two-year-
old exchange student from Germany touring the Eastern seaboard,
marched herself barefoot right up to the Stoltzfus's front door, rapped
on it, and boldly declared in broken half-English, half-German, "I
am from Germany, and I would like to see an Amish house."*

*Because Elam and Rachel relish a certain kind of directness and
audacity, and because they delight in being astonished, they opened
their doors for the first time to an "outsider." Anette practically became the Stoltzfus's daughter for the summer—and for life. In the
middle of Anette's stay, Rachel "stitched" her an Amish dress, and
Anette began to accompany the rest of Elam and Rachel's children in
the back of the gray-topped market wagon whenever they all trooped
up the Belmont Road to a neighbor's farm for church. None of the
Amish in Elam and Rachel's church district ever really inquired as to
who Anette was since, after all, there she sat with the Stoltzfus girls
wearing her Amish dress, and she could speak German after a couple
of weeks in a way that approximated Pennsylvania Dutch. "People
figured she was a cousin or something," Rachel says laughing while
she cleans the lettuce she has just plucked from her garden in back of
the house.*

*"And imagine! This crazy girl walked here the next year from the
Lancaster train station (a distance of about thirteen miles) on a snowy*

Christmas Eve and banged on our door in the middle of the night with Christmas presents for all of us under both arms!"

◆

At forty, Anette Scherer has arrived again, this time with her own two children, Oliver, nine, and Verity, five, as well as her niece and namesake, Anette, a German medical student doing a residency at the Hershey, Pennsylvania, Medical Center. They are on their way back to Anette Senior's home (and husband) in Nebraska.

I pull the repaired Horizon into the Stoltzfus drive at 5:00 P.M. and seat myself amidst catching-up stories and merriment. Like a daughter, Anette helps Rachel prepare supper, still knowing which cabinet to open for a salad bowl, a plate, or a saucepan.

Anette knows well the ins and outs of the Stoltzfus house. She bustles about so that her frizzy brown ponytail bobbles as she helps Rachel cut up crisp vegetables, all the while taking care of Oliver and Verity, saying something, first in English to Rachel, and then translating into German for Anette Junior. I am glad for the presence of the two Anettes because now, during a time of so many stories, the story of my arrival makes for a good telling and removes both for Rachel and me the strangeness of being alone with each other in so big a house.

When I finish telling about all the tourist goings on in Intercourse and how glad I am to be back with a car that works, Rachel turns from the sink suddenly and says, her eyes flashing, "Well, you know what they say: a bad beginning makes a good finish. Let's hope so." And I feel my whole being reach for this comment that seems aimed right at my heart—a challenge and an expectation.

Rachel takes me up the creaky wooden stairs to what will be my room for the summer. When we get to the top of the stairs she turns to me saying, "Every one of your people who comes to us wants something. So what is it *you* want?"

I reel at such a direct question. I mumble something about writing a thesis for school. The Stoltzfuses have chosen to know enough about the outside world that they know what a thesis is. And, like many Amish men, as a would-be historian and genealogist, Elam has had more than occasional dealings with university people, historians, archivists, scholars—even the librarians at the Library of Congress in Washington. In the past, the Stoltzfuses have even had one other graduate student stay with them.

But this answer doesn't satisfy Rachel. She could not care less about writing. Privately she believes "people on the outside go to school too much" anyway. Rachel also knows that on a day-to-day basis, she will be the one to deal with me more directly, as is her way. So she tries another equally direct tack, "Are you satisfied with your own religion?"

I look her right in the eye. This is a *very* important question for both of us, and I know what's behind it. John Hostetler had told me about the hordes of souls regularly coming to the Amish in hopes of being what Rachel calls "converts"—people trying to fill an unfillable void in their own lives. Rachel and Elam have had more than their share of lost ones coming to them for something they know is not theirs to offer.

So I answer truthfully but quietly. "I am a happy Catholic."

"Well, GOOD! I just wanted to make sure," Rachel says. Then she bounces back down the stairs to her company with a lighter, relieved gait that is as palpable as sunlight in the meadow.

◆

Dusk.

I am sitting at the wooden desk in what is to be my room for the summer, on the second floor over the sitting room. From over the rollers of the typewriter I can look out of two windows, their white lace curtains quivering at any faint trace of evening breeze. From the window in front of me I can see the Belmont Road as it dips toward and then past the Stoltzfus farm—the same road I traveled in a daze twelve hours ago. From the other I regard dark brown mules across the road, gathered at the creek, as if recounting their day as I now am mine.

The sky is creamy violet. Buried behind sheets of filmy cloud is a dull white candle-flame sun. Levi is in the field cutting alfalfa with a long blade pulled by two mules named Hans and Dot. Rachel and the

two Anettes are chattering away in German and Dutch, still at the kitchen table. I listen to their voices as they blend with the birds chirping in the meadow, an occasional cow mooing, and the wwhhoosshh of a camper as it heads back up the hill toward Intercourse. Elam is with three of his Amish friends. They have gone to research family records.

Rachel has given me a box of safety matches and shown me how to light the glass hurricane lamp on the dresser without setting the whole house on fire.

"You city people don't know how to do anything," she says, socking me playfully in the side after my first attempt at lighting the lamp sends a pillar of fire straight into the air. "Turn the wick way down. You just want to barely touch it with the match. See? Like this."

Rachel also gives me a red plastic flashlight with which to negotiate the squeaky wooden stairs to the basement toilet in the middle of the night. It will take two weeks before I stop feeling the wall with my flattened palm for a light switch and remember to bring the flashlight during my regular midnight descents.

The alarm clock reads 6:50 and the setting sun is almost directly in my eyes. The chrome on the typewriter looks gold. "Every one of your people who comes to us wants something. So what is it you want?"

I type Rachel's words and they sit on the page like an exclamation point.

◆

Later in the evening Levi and I drive to a farm outside the town of Gap, a hamlet and truckstop known for its goofy wooden town clock that looks like a stranded lighthouse. Levi wants to look at a horse he saw advertised in a weekly farm paper.

Once there, Levi and the other Amishman speak Dutch while I sit in the Horizon watching the man's two little girls, barefoot, in gray dresses, as they play among the horses in their wooden stalls. I find myself worrying about them as they stand directly behind the horses' rear legs. But then one of the horses turns to the littlest girl and pushes her gently with his head, teasing her as she giggles.

Then we pick up Elam at a farm just outside Lancaster, not far from Dutch Wonderland. He is sitting outside in the cooling summer air.

24

At nine-thirty "fast time" (the Amish do not advance their clocks in the spring and call outside world time "fast time" and their own time "slow time") Levi, Elam, and I are driving down Route 340 for Paradise. I tell them about a man named Clare Hamilton who drives a surrey full of tourists through Intercourse pulled by two beautiful black mares saying, "Sixty-five miles from Intercourse to Philadelphia, SIXTY-FIVE TAVERNS ALL ALONG THE WAY: the FIRST gave Intercourse its original name!" He speaks as if his passengers were standing outside a canvas tent about to watch the bearded lady swallow a sword of fire.

"That's a bunch of baloney," Elam says laughing. "You'll have to read an article by Abraham Blank about the earliest days of Intercourse. I'll show it to you some time."

When we pull into the Stoltzfus driveway, the house is silent. Levi's dairy cows stir in the barn. A cow moos distantly over the next ridge. It is startling to me how few lights are on. But for the outside lights from a local public school down the road, the night is blackness and fog.

As we enter the house I see that Rachel has left a hurricane lamp with "Home Sweet Home" etched on it burning on the stove, and Elam gives me a flashlight and I make my way up the steep stairs to my room where another lamp has been lit and the covers have been pulled back and Elam says "Weeellll. Good night," like Agee's sharecroppers, and I hear the springs under his and Rachel's bed give with his weight and then Elam lets out a huge yawn that hangs over the house for a minute as if all the work in his soul has been let loose for the few brief hours when he and Rachel finally, finally turn to each other in the black foggy silence of the country and close their eyes and sleep.

The next morning, Pentecost Sunday, Paradise, PA. *Pentecost.* From the Latin word for "fifty." Fifty days after Jesus' death; the day the Apostles of Jesus were given wisdom in the form of tongues of fire that hovered above their heads when they were gathered together behind locked doors.

It is 6:00 A.M. I know I should get up, but the bed I am in is so comfortable and the two blue quilts that I hug to my chest are so enveloping that I cannot. I listen to Elam, Rachel, and the two Anettes speaking English and German and I can smell coffee and toasted bread and I think, "Here you are lying in bed just like the city boy Rachel said you are," but I am so exhausted from the trek to get here and its emotional intensity that I wish I could sleep for another decade.

With my hair standing straight up and rumply clothes thrown on, I nevertheless negotiate the squeaky wooden steps feeling pasty and unshaven.

"Good morning!" comes a collective sing-song from the table the minute I hit the landing. The greeting is like having a bucket of ice water thrown at me. But to sit down at the Stoltzfus breakfast table—awake or not—is to dive right into life.

"So what about the horse?" Rachel asks, turning from the stove where she is fixing me two eggs, Amish-style, cooked in margarine and warm milk.

"What horse?" I ask, sounding hung over.

"Why, the horse you and Levi looked at last night!"

"Oh, that horse!" I blurt out and everyone starts laughing. And thank God I remember and tell about the first horse that the man showed Levi and that the better horse—the one Levi *really* liked—was the second one he showed, a three-year-old which stood about two hands above tall, tall Levi, but which had already been reserved by another Amishman.

Elam is in his chair—a metal office chair on casters, a regular feature of every Amish home I visit—with old leather-bound books he has pulled from his study spread out in front of him, surrounding his breakfast, which he has hardly touched, which undoes Rachel.

"Here's today's Scripture for Pentecost," Elam says, handing Anette Junior a German Bible. (German, not Pennsylvania Dutch, is the language read in Amish church.) "Do you think you can read this?"

"Ja! Ja!" Anette says as Elam slides the book to her, and then he gives me an English Bible so I can follow along.

So far Anette Junior has been wide-eyed but quiet. But something in Elam seems to know that this is what she has been waiting for. Now, as Anette reads, there is discovery, while her long, thin doctor's hands cradle her brown hair at her forehead.

Stillness.

The whole farm seems to stop as Anette reads the first two chapters from the Acts of the Apostles:

"You will receive power when the Holy Spirit comes down on you; then you are to be my witnesses in Jerusalem, throughout Judea and Samaria, yes even to the ends of the earth." No sooner had He said this than He was lifted up before their eyes in a cloud which took Him from their sight. . . .

And when the day of Pentecost came it found them gathered in one place. Suddenly from up in the sky there came a noise like a strong, driving wind which was heard all through the house where they were seated. Tongues as of fire appeared, which parted and came to rest on each of them. All were filled with the Holy Spirit.

Silence.

In a whisper, Elam says, "You done a real good job, Anette." His eyes are brimming with gratitude. Anette's shimmer. I look away for a moment. Two of Levi's mules are rolling around in the dust of the pasture along the creek.

"Now come on, Dad! Time to GO!" Rachel says with exaggerated bossiness, which makes everybody laugh, as she has intended.

"When Mum says it's time to go, it's time to GO!" Elam sighs.

In the next breath the two are walking down the Belmont Road—Rachel in her black dress, formal black bonnet, Elam in his blousey white shirt, straw hat, black vest and pants, his beard and hair plastered down by Rachel with water. Rachel walks slightly ahead of Elam. Her step is more lively than Elam's. They will arrive at their neighbor's house for church a half hour early. They are always early.

(Church for the Amish is held in the home. There is no church building. Amish families in a given church district take turns holding service and serving a light meal afterward.)

Later, Levi, Katie holding the baby, then Benuel and Rebecca come out of the other side of the house, dressed the same. Benuel and Rebecca are barefoot. Benuel scratches his rear end as he walks. Levi, Katie, and their young family are always late.

The rest of us, now joined by Oliver and Verity, remain at the kitchen table watching Amish buggies arrive and turn into the Lapps' driveway, which is bordered by a curving, white wooden fence. Oliver wants to go for a walk. So Anette and her niece pack a lunch while I jump in the car and buy some iced tea at the PENN SUPREME convenience store in Intercourse.

At a little after eight o'clock slow time the five of us are walking: the countryside is hushed but for the rhythm of Amish buggies on the way to services in their own or neighboring districts. At this time of day you can understand Lancaster County's deep religiosity—when the Amish are one, assembled across the County for prayer. As we walk by, we can see all the women sitting on benches along the windows in the Lapps' house. There is a kind of monotone singing that melds with the rhythm of horse hooves on asphalt.

The farms are all deserted. Dogs come running to greet us at the road: two sets of collies on two separate farms. We watch an old water wheel and the plud-thoosh, plud-thoosh it makes as it rhythmically turns while its wires move in a line guided by squeaking wooden poles all the way to the yard of the house. We see a cow with a deep cleft in her lip from a burn. The cow knows we are staring at her; she looks at us and then looks away and then back at us as if to say, "So now you've seen me. Go away and stop staring."

Later in the morning, at another farm, Amish boys are waiting outside to go back in the farmhouse to eat while the women prepare food and set the table. They sit on the long white fence along the driveway. From where we are, at least a hundred yards away, the casual arms slung and the easy bodies leaning in black and white slouches make them look like crows on a wire. There are at least twenty boys.

When we get back, Elam and Rachel have returned from church. We spend the better part of the afternoon and far into the evening talking. Elam takes us into his study to see his collection of German Bibles, and Rachel puts me on the gravity-inversion system, saying, "I try to get on the stretcher a couple of times a week! Dad doesn't like to get on so much but I make him—it's good for you."

Elam pulls a German version of the *Lives of the Saints* down from the high shelves in his study and brings it to the kitchen table. Anette Junior reads from it slowly, translating into English. "This book is, what is the word? Flowery! It is too much the way it is written—*too* nice, I think," she tells Elam.

"You're probably right," he says. "After all, the thing that makes a saint is the struggle, when you wrestle with your faith."

We all stay up later than we should. Oliver and Verity have gone to bed. The room is now lit by the propane lamp on a stand with wheels, which is in the middle of the room.

Elam gets up and decides *he'll* serve everybody ice cream. He gets a Tupperware box out of the top of the refrigerator and an ice cream scooper, five plates, and a couple of spoons. Then he sits down! So *I* stand up.

"Good! Now the men can serve us!" Rachel says, laughing. This is a big laugh in this world. The men hardly ever go near anything connected with food, dishes, plates, or stoves.

I open up the container—chunky gray matter that, possibly, a hundred years ago could once have been ice cream. I put the scooper in. Cement.

I taste it. "Ugh! This is *chicken!*"

Rachel laughs so hard she starts coughing. Elam sits smiling like a schoolboy caught with his pants down.

More stories. About disciplining children. I tell about a little girl in the first third grade class I ever taught. Despite silver stars licked onto charts made with green magic markers, rewards, and so on, this little girl loved to run up the stairs ahead of all her classmates from recess. And as the rest walked upstairs to my classroom, she wedged her blond head between the rungs of the great banister at the top of the stairs and spat great gobs of spit onto her classmates while they cried for me to come and see.

Elam and Rachel are wide-eyed. They turn and look at each other. I continue. After weeks of trying everything—calling the child's mother and father, scolding her, being gentle with her, putting a gold star on a chart whenever she had a day without spitting, I caught her one day, ready to fire. So *I* spat right in her face like a camel and said, "There! How do you like it?"

I conclude the story saying, "And that was the end of the spitting!"

Elam laughs so hard his rocker almost tips over. Rachel goes into another coughing fit. "You didn't?!" she says to me.

"I did! I didn't know what else to do! But it worked!"

Elam and Rachel look at each other again, as if this story is what they have been waiting to hear, as if to say, "He'll be fine, he's got some fire in him."

29

◆

Pentecost is celebrated by the Amish for two days. So from the earliest hours of Monday morning, Elam and Rachel have company from among their ten married daughters and sons and their forty-eight grandchildren. When I lumber down the stairs the kitchen table is lengthened by mismatched wooden leaves and set for twelve. Once again I wish I could appear with a paper bag over my head, until I've had a cup of coffee.

Miriam, the second-oldest of "Rachel's girls," her husband, Levi Petersheim, and their nine children are all seated. When I step down from the landing and turn the corner into the sitting room, I am regarded by the Petersheim children as if I have stepped out of a spaceship. I smile, but my heart is pounding. "This is Randy, everybody," Rachel announces.

Another chair is fetched. We bow our heads, hands in our laps, as the Amish do before every meal. A prayerfully long silence. I listen to traffic; to Amos, Becca, and Isaac, Miriam and Levi's littlest children, breathing through their mouths; to Shorty's toenails clicking across the kitchen. The silence is broken by a deep sigh from Elam as he leans backward in his gray office chair, causing it to squeak.

We eat a tremendously filling breakfast consisting of eggs cooked in milk and margarine, beets, soda crackers with hot milk poured over them, and pancakes in heavy syrup and thank God there is instant coffee. As we eat I think, "They eat this way because they work so hard."

The meal is mostly eaten in silence since the Petersheims probably left their house at about five to drive up here from Quarryville. They all look groggy. It is now seven thirty, slow time. Rachel orchestrates the entire roomful of people: who should sit where and how the food gets passed from one end of the long table to the other. Her sharp eyes anticipate my skittishness in reaching for a plate of pancakes or the jar of beets. Part of me burns that I can't fend for myself in this world, grateful nonetheless that Rachel is so astute. Then the two Anettes, Oliver, and Verity come downstairs to the table and once again chairs are fetched, the group expands, and the food winds its way around the table.

Right after breakfast, I take Levi in the Horizon to a chiropractor for a back treatment. Anette Junior accompanies us. When we return, two more of Rachel and Elam's children, Savilla and Jacob, their spouses, Henry and Mary, and their eight children have arrived. Now three teams are hitched to the metal hitching post just outside the barn where the lane turns to head into the fields.

The room is split right down the middle—the table has expanded yet again and is now set for over thirty. The women chop asparagus at the sink, take cakes out of Tupperware containers, wipe children's noses, and wash lettuce, with the two Anettes weaving in and out the entire time. I watch the three daughters recounting the various times when Anette stayed with the Stoltzfuses. There is a pause and then, "Oh. OH! ANETTE!" and then a flurry of very animated Dutch.

Elam, Levi, Jake, and Henry sit in the sitting room, as do I. They speak Dutch the entire time. During this waiting time as the women prepare the food I feel like the cow we saw in the meadow yesterday. Henry Beiler, one of Elam's sons-in-law, has a big round face and hard features, looking to me like a gangster in disguise. Elam calls him "a man's man." Jake is tall and gawky. He turns to me and says, "Are you Deutsch?"

"Me? No. I'm from Boston."

"Oh, you're an Englishman."

I smile a gooney smile and twirl around and around the copy of *David Copperfield* I am holding in my hand. Every time I swallow I am aware of doing so.

Just before everyone sits down, Benuel comes through Elam's study from the other side of the house, waddling through the gathering in his blue underpants. Rachel says something to him sternly in Dutch. The older girls giggle. Benuel runs off and returns a moment later—dressed—with Rebecca and his mother and father.

The Amish eat their big meal, dinner, at about eleven. I look at the striking assemblage in which I sit: men in their cobalt blue shirts, black vests and pants, the women all in navy and white. I watch the children help each other out at the table. I watch the women in the kitchen and the men talking, waiting to eat, and I see how order and clarity define this community.

But it's hard to go beyond the visual picture. With the language barrier, with the sameness present everywhere, subtlety is absent for me. It is too easy for me to remove from the Amish their core humanity, the particulars of lives and relationships.

"Just like the tourists," I think to myself.

As we finish dinner, we watch a group of tourists in a blue Ford Escort stop their car and get out to take pictures of Holsteins. An Amish market wagon passes. The people take a picture of the buggy as it passes by, then jump in their car and follow it down the road, a video camera hanging out the right side. Rachel looks at the two Anettes and me, saying, "Happens all the time."

◆

The two Anettes are leaving. They have been buffers to ease my transition from one world to another. And they are friends. Anette Senior walks with me up the field lane.

"Do you have any advice?" I ask her, hopeful, frightened, and heartbroken.

"The Stoltzfuses are very direct people," Anette begins. "They appreciate help more than anything. Do things without being asked. And whatever you do, do it as best you can. They know you're not a farmer, but extra hands really can help out. Effort goes a long long way among the Amish. And appreciate them! They are the kindest people I have ever met. I hope that what happened to me will happen to you."

Anette Junior hugs me. "Write well. Remember everything," is her bald advice. And then she and Anette Senior and Oliver and Verity get in their Volkswagen Rabbit and go beeping up the hill toward Route 30.

I stand for a moment in the driveway and hear the animated Dutch chatter of the extended Stoltzfus family in the sitting room. Going back in the house, I excuse myself from the table, feeling absolutely foreign and more lonely than I have ever felt in my life.

PART FIVE

By the sweat of your brow shall you get

bread to eat. —Genesis 3:19

◆

I set the alarm clock each night for 4:45 A.M. But it will take two months to get over my complete disorientation when the alarm goes off in what feels like the middle of the night.

◆

At 5:00 A.M. every morning, across Lancaster County, whether in bleary drizzle or stifling heat, the diesel generators start up and the milking begins. The chugging of hundreds of generators in Amish barns makes early morning chamber music. Since the Amish will not use electricity, the diesels provide power for automatic milking machines. They also power the tubular suction system that draws hot, steamy 99-degree milk from the black and white Holsteins lined up in their stalls at one end of the barn to the cooling tanks in the milk house far at the other end.

Down Meadowbrook Road, Benuel King's generator is tuned lower than Levi's; its chugs have more space and air between them. Across the Belmont Road, Aaron Lapp's is high and whiny; farther down the road, Amos Petersheim's generator purrs like a new German roadster.

Levi and Katie wander sleepily out of their side of the house with their thirteen-year-old "hired man," Amos King. He walks behind

Katie and Levi, tucking his brown shirt into his suspendered pants. Levi goes to the generator and flips a toggle switch. Katie fetches three stainless-steel milking cans from the "milk house." It contains a 400-gallon, stainless-steel cooling tank that brings the temperature of the milk down to 40 degrees within a matter of minutes. While Levi and Katie head for the barn, Amos heads for the meadow.

Levi Stoltzfus is at any given time milking about thirty-five Holsteins, each of which will produce about 17,500 pounds of milk per year. There are approximately 1,000 Amish farms in Lancaster County, the great majority of which are dairy farms like Levi's. Lancaster County is the fifth-largest dairy-producing county in the United States.

The Holsteins bawl impatiently at the gate closest to the rear entrance of the barn. Eminently creatures of habit, the cows know it is time to be fed—sweet, moist, fermented corn silage and a ladleful of dry crunchy grain. Their udders are pathetically full, and part of the reason the cows moo with such insistence is for the sweet release of pressure provided by the gently pulsating nozzles of the vacuum-type milking machines. The cows have spent the night lolling and grazing at the far end of the meadow. Amos opens the electrified fence and the cows charge in.

With their lumbering bodies, long thin legs, and cleft hooves, I tell Levi his cows look like fat ladies stuffed into high-heeled shoes. Blank-faced, they are the quintessence of comic haughtiness. Walking in by way of a cement ramp, they might be contestants in some hilarious beauty pageant for the goofy and the vain.

"But really, if you stop and think about it," Levi explains while he and Katie wash the cows' udders with soapy cloths and then attach the suction nozzles to them, "the real beauty of a cow is the machinery on the inside. When you think that all these things eat is the corn we grow, grain, water, and some alfalfa—and then they give us milk back in return—well, no matter how ornery they are, we kinda have to be grateful to them. They give us our bread and butter."

Of course, I think. My metaphors express only my lack of comprehension.

Levi, Katie, and Amos work methodically as a team, milking and feeding the cows. Katie and Levi move down the stalls one by one. Amos shovels silage from a wooden feed cart into the cows' feeding troughs or breaks up bales of alfalfa, to be stuffed into the larger calves' mangers.

Already at 6:00 A.M., it is 78 degrees and humid. Levi and Katie are both barefoot, and Levi's shirt is unbuttoned to his pants. Katie speaks animatedly in Dutch, her brown eyes flashing. Every now and then she drops her voice to a gutteral tone, urging a stubborn cow to make room for the milking apparatus.

In this summer of 1988 there will be no substantial rainfall until the middle of July. There will be only constant, draining humidity.

Benuel has awakened. He wanders from the house toward the barn in his underpants and his father's boots, and carries a gray kitten he has snatched from its hiding place beneath the floorboards of the porch.

I am astonished, sweeping the barn floor, by how dirty cows are. While milking goes on, cow after cow lifts its long tail, releasing a long, light-brown stream into a trough running the length of the barn directly behind the stanchions. But like all things in Amish life, manure is vital to the farm. Levi and Amos shovel it up and empty it into a manure pit in a far corner of the barn. It will be spread on the fields for fertilizer.

This morning, as every morning, the barn smells of silage, cow flops, warm milk, and straw. The blend of smells is beautiful, radiating activity, life.

Levi opens up one of the milk cans and pours the hot milk into a bent skillet. Instantly fourteen cats and their kittens come running from everywhere, greedily lapping up the milk. Some of the smaller kitties become so excited they climb right into the pan.

By 7:00 A.M., as in all the barns around us, the cows have been milked, the manure trough emptied, and the cows and heifers fed and let back out to pasture.

"Being a dairy farmer keeps you close to home," Levi reflects one morning at the breakfast table. "No matter what you do during the day, you have to be home by five for milking and up by five the next morning to do it all over again."

35

Once I asked Levi what he'd be if he weren't an Amish dairy farmer. He drew on his pipe slowly. "I guess I'd like to be a trucker. Then I could go all across the United States—see the whole country—but still have a place I could call home."

◆

In his second term in office, Ronald Reagan paid American dairy farmers to slaughter their herds of cattle. The reason cited was a milk surplus. Many farmers complied. Over a million dairy cattle were destroyed in less than a year's time.

The Amish, of course, refused. Suspicious of the notion of a farm surplus and horrified by the thought of the destruction of their farm animals, they chose instead to pay a mandatory tariff of one dollar on every hundred pounds of milk produced.

The Amish call this "the milk tax." In their view, they are paying the federal government in order to maintain their way of life as dairy farmers in Lancaster County.

◆

Later in the day, we walk to the barn to give the cows some feed. While shoveling the dry, grainy mixture from a wooden silage cart, Levi looks at his herd sympathetically. "We have to work these things harder and harder these days on less and less land," he reflects. "I do things with my herd my father would never have done. NEVER. They fed their herds a lot more hay than we do, for one thing, because they had the fields and they didn't have as many cows on them. My cows' stomachs get twisted much more than they did when my father was farming. Because they're working too hard. A cow could hold up longer. There's just no way my sons will be able to farm here unless things soon change."

This thought bothers Levi. His usually-smooth shoveling is now rough and jerky. "There is just no way," he says again.

PART SIX

And they that were not written into the Book
of Life were cast into a lake of fire.

—Revelation 20:15

◆

Route 340, heading toward Lancaster.

White Amish farmhouses on the left. Two Holstein cows stand near a billboard on the right: VISIT THE AMISH VILLAGE. TURN LEFT ON 896. *Another billboard.* THE AMISH BARN: GOOD FOOD AND SHOPPING FUN. *Another.* MILLER'S SMORGASBORD. *Another.* STRASBURG RAILROAD: THE TRAIN TO PARADISE. *And another.* MT. HOPE WINE GALLERY. *And another.* STOLTZFUS FARM RESTAURANT: FAMILY STYLE MEALS. *And another and another and another and another and another. A bus shelter along Route 340 reads:* WHO ARE THE AMISH? FIND OUT: THE PEOPLE'S PLACE. INTERCOURSE. STRAIGHT AHEAD. *An Amish grandfather dressed in "city blacks" sits with his grandson beneath the advertisement, waiting for the Number 13 bus from White Horse to Lancaster. Further down the road, tucked behind a thicket of tall pine trees stands another sign. Unless one knew its location, it would otherwise remain obscured. The billboard is shaped like an opened Bible. It stands about a hundred yards away from* THE AMISH BARN, *a restaurant and gift shop with an adjoining miniature-golf course near a one-room Amish schoolhouse.*

The Scriptural citation on the billboard has all but faded away, but the quote itself is still legible.

"AND THEY THAT WERE NOT WRITTEN INTO THE BOOK OF LIFE WERE CAST INTO A LAKE OF FIRE."

38

PART SEVEN

How can the earthen pot go with the metal

cauldron? When they knock together,

the pot will be smashed . . .

—Sirach 13:2

◆

5:30 A.M. Route 41, Christiana, PA.

   On a quiet Sunday morning in June, Levi and Katie King and their five daughters, all of Atglen, are in their gray-topped buggy heading to church. Suddenly a drunk driver slams into the rear of the carriage. On impact, all seven members of the King family are thrown over an embankment into a ditch. The cab of the buggy separates from the frame, spinning to rest on the opposite side of the road. The Kings are found under wreckage from the buggy, and police discover their horse lying dead in a field near the scene of the accident. (Later, witnesses testify that the buggy was visible for miles before it was hit.) All five of the King children suffer broken legs. Their mother, Katie, thirty-seven, has a miscarriage and loses her spleen. Levi King, thirty-eight, is permanently paralyzed from the neck down.

   The driver doesn't stop, but is later arrested when a state trooper, heading for the accident, sees him assessing his damaged van a few miles away. Upon his arrest twenty-four-year-old Marcial Chavez snaps, "Man, those are stupid people. They didn't even try to get out of my way. Do you know how much it's going to cost to fix my van?"

40

Chavez is sentenced to two-years-less-one-day to five-years-less-one-day in the Lancaster County Prison. At sentencing, an outraged Judge Louise G. Herr (whose sentence is six months short of the maximum penalty) berates Chavez's defense attorney, Robert Reese, for advising Chavez not to make contact with the King family.

"That was a cold-hearted suggestion," Herr scolds Reese, "couldn't you have contacted the victims on behalf of your client?" *

◆

As of this writing, there are over 300,000 motor vehicles registered in Lancaster County. This compares with approximately 185,000 in 1970. Since the 1970s, plans have been on the drawing board for some sort of new highway through Lancaster County in order to link the Harrisburg/York area with Philadelphia. Although the Pennsylvania Turnpike crosses the northern edge of the county, it isn't as widely used as it might be; truckers don't like to pay the tolls, and county residents prefer to wind their way around it using an intricate network of narrower county roads. The Amish prefer the backroads too, for obvious reasons.

A steadily rising number of automobiles in Lancaster County has added congestion—and accidents—to two key throughways in particular: Routes 30 and 23. One can travel Route 30 in patches of varying width and condition from Philadelphia to Lancaster. Past the hamlet of Gap, at the eastern end of Lancaster County, Amish farms and houses along Route 30 suddenly give way to Rockvale Center, a conglomeration of some ninety outlet stores behind which are numerous Amish farms and houses; chain hotels like the Sheraton and MacIntosh Inn; a K-Mart; McDonald's, Burger King, and other fast-food franchises; shopping centers and tourist attractions with names like "Dutch Wonderland," and the steamboat-shaped "Robert Fulton Inn." (The latter pipes tape-recorded seagull noises into its parking lots while Route 30's traffic roars past its neon paddle wheel.)

Route 23, a two-lane road that travels all the way from Lancaster through Valley Forge National Park in suburban Chester County, is

---

* Adapted from: Drybred, John, "Amish Family Injured when Buggy Struck," *The Lancaster Intelligencer Journal*, June 27, 1988, page 1, and "Hit-run Driver Gets Jail Term for Buggy Crash," *The Lancaster Intelligencer Journal*, February 2, 1989.

still predominantly residential or rural, until it reaches the borough of New Holland. There it becomes lined with factories, convenience stores, gas stations, strip malls, and recently built tract housing.

When they occur, automobile-buggy accidents on both roads are especially harrowing, given the amount of traffic on them and their posted speed limits. This is especially true for Route 30.

As a rule the Amish avoid both roads, but in several key places they must cross them or travel on them for a stretch. Till recently I knew of only two yellow signs denoting horse-and-buggy traffic posted on Lancaster County roads. Such signs are common, however, in Mifflin and Somerset Counties, areas where the number of Amish is much smaller than in Lancaster County. The Pennsylvania Department of Transportation (PENNDoT) and local officials claim the Amish don't want the signs posted because they would draw further attention to their presence in Lancaster County.

In September 1987 PENNDoT announced it would hold a public hearing to present plans for a highway involving Routes 30 and 23, in order to ease mounting county-wide traffic congestion. The new corridor, called the "Route 30 Bypass" (a four-lane superhighway), would bisect the Amish heartland.

On learning of the proposal and hearing (publicly announced two weeks before it was to take place), Richard Armstrong, an airline pilot living outside of Intercourse, along with two Amish neighbors and another English friend, quickly distributed leaflets throughout the Amish community announcing the hearing. The national media were also alerted, and they said they would certainly be there. The question was, would the Amish?

On the night of the hearing, scores of gray-topped buggies rumbled down Route 772 and began pulling into the parking lot of Pequea Valley High School, a large, red-brick institution recently built on land Amish farmers were pressured into selling to the town. The *Wall Street Journal*, National Public Radio, and the local press were all on hand.

Outside, the parking lot began to fill early with an odd mixture of buggies and cars. The auditorium, with seating for only 750, filled quickly, and the gathering crowd stood patiently outside, chatting away. This was, after all, a fortuitous circumstance allowing a large segment of the Amish community to catch up with friends they perhaps had not seen in a good while. Recounting the events of the evening later, Richard Armstrong observed, "The atmosphere outside was like an Amish wedding."

PENNDoT officials, watching the arriving Amish multitude, were not as jovial. Some expressed concern that the Amish might riot— an absurd proposition to anybody with the slightest understanding of the Amish. No one, not PENNDoT, not local officials, not the Lancaster City newspapers, least of all Richard Armstrong and his friends, ever anticipated such a large turnout. Over a thousand Amish and five hundred of their English neighbors showed up.

There was some quick regrouping by PENNDoT officials in order to accommodate the throng; after several minutes of confusion, they decided that proceedings should take place in two sessions.

Anxious Amishmen craned their necks into the auditorium holding their straw hats in their hands, and Amish women sat quietly, hands folded in their laps, some with children present. Well-dressed PENNDoT officials spoke in bland technical jargon about "corridors" and proposed "phases of construction" and presented transparencies showing wide blue arrows obliterating the area inhabited by the people in the audience.

At the end of the first session, Richard Armstrong stood up and asked PENNDoT official Robert Mueser from the audience, "Will there be additional hearings on the highway, or is this it?" Mueser glanced over at his colleagues, then said something about scheduling. Armstrong repeated the question twice, and twice again he was told about shortened project "time lines." When Mueser asked if there were any other questions, Armstrong, still on his feet, turned to the overflow crowd and asked, "Will all those present concerned about the impact of a new highway on Lancaster County please stand?"

There was a long, awkward silence. People glanced at one another, and then, Amish and English alike, the room rose to its feet.*

* In the second session, Armstrong again asked the question, and again the room of 750 took to its feet.

44

The hearing galvanized national opposition to the highway. It was the first time in the history of Lancaster County that the Amish had attended a hearing in such numbers. For the media, the contrast was stark and obvious—simple, agrarian people listening silently while state bureaucrats with voices void of affect spoke about actions that would destroy the Plain Sect communities. One reporter characterized the hearing as "a sweetheart story."

Letters from across the country flooded Governor Casey's office. In a report John Hostetler wrote for the Commonwealth concerning the highway's impact on the Amish, he said he believed that many Amish, suddenly separated from their families by the highway, would probably move away. He underscored the unique cultural and moral contribution of the Amish to the Commonwealth by citing a portion of Chief Justice Warren Burger's 1972 opinion upholding the Amish right to maintain their own parochial schools:

"We must not forget," Burger admonished, "that in the Middle Ages, important values of the civilization of the Western world were preserved by members of religious orders who isolated themselves from all worldly influences against great obstacles. There can be no assumption that today's majority is 'right' and the Amish and others like them are 'wrong.'"*

Bowing to national public pressure, Transportation Secretary Howard Yerusalim announced in January 1988, "I have reviewed the preliminary findings of the study with Governor Casey, and he has determined that we will not build a new highway in any corridor that will bisect the Amish farming community or cause a major disruption to the Amish lifestyle."

It seemed as if the threat of a highway was gone.

In September of the same year Amish families in Lancaster County were surprised to receive a newsletter from PENNDoT with the innocuous title: "Traffic Relief Route Environmental Study Update." The newsletter's contents, however, were anything but innocuous. It outlined, among other things, the resurrection of an

---

*Lestz, Gerald, final chapter of *Amish Perspectives*, York Graphic Services: York, Pa., 1989, pages 100–101. *Wisconsin* v. *Yoder et al.*, U.S. Supreme Court, Number 7-110. Argued December 8, 1971; decided May 15, 1972.

45

idea floating around the county since the mid-1970s: relocation and expansion of Route 23.

In particular, responding to pressure from the Lancaster Chamber of Commerce, the Lancaster business community, and many state lawmakers, the newsletter advocated the completion of a stretch of the highway from just outside Lancaster City to Leola. The section had been graded in 1974–75 and interchanges were built, but when statewide highway funding dried up, the project was abandoned. The land was then rented back to the farmers from whom it had been originally purchased under eminent domain. The farmers put their cattle out to pasture on it, and the unfinished stretch became known laughably among farmers as the "goat path."

Support for the completion of the "goat path" and further modernization of Route 23 was also fueled by Ford Motor Company's recent relocation of its farm equipment division to the city of New Holland, which sits along old Route 23. An expanded highway would allow Ford to ship out its equipment much more easily.

This proposal was recommended, even though the newsletter noted: "The study area is dominated by active agricultural land, most of which has strong cultural traditions. The large Amish settlement and other Plain Sect groups within the study area have contributed greatly in maintaining the study area as one of the most productive farming districts in the country. The farming techniques used today are in many cases the same as they were two hundred years ago."

Then there is this observation, one whose directness seems lost in an otherwise obtuse technical document: "In many respects, the study area's traditions and culture depend on the farmlands' existence." *

At a PENNDoT hearing held early in March 1989 to discuss the proposed plans for Route 23, a citizens' action group opposed to the new road was on hand. Fifty of its number included Amish and Mennonite farmers. A spokeswoman for the group asked those opposed to the highway to stand, and the Plain Sect peoples joined their English neighbors. When a spokesman for another citizens' group

* "Traffic Relief Route Environmental Study Update," published by the Pennsylvania Department of Transportation: Harrisburg, Pa., September 1988, Number 4.

then quoted Governor Casey's promise, Howard Yerusalim assured those in attendance that Casey's word was still good.

At another March meeting in Harrisburg between Plain Sect farmers, local citizens' groups, and PENNDoT, Yerusalim reiterated the Governor's promise for a third time: no new highway "will bisect the Amish farming community."

However, the matter is far from settled. PENNDoT recently commissioned a $600,000 "cultural-impact study," the purported goal of which was to assess the cultural effects of a new or widened Route 23 on the nearby Plain Sect communities.

In February 1991 Abraham Blank, an Amish elder who sometimes writes for Amish periodicals, was visited by a consultant for the PENNDoT study named Watt Bowie. Bowie told Blank that where a new Route 23 is concerned, "This time PENNDoT means business."

State Senator Noah Wenger, an ex-farmer and past President of the Pennsylvania Farmers' Association, testified in March 1991 in support of a new Route 23 before the State Transportation Commission in Chambersburg, Pennsylvania. In his testimony, Wenger blasted land-preservation groups for their opposition to the road.

As Wenger sees it, new highways must be built for the farm-related industries around the New Holland area, including the Ford New Holland farm machinery and Tyson Foods plants. He believes that if both companies (formerly owned by county families) have difficulty moving their products out of Lancaster County, they will move away. Ford Motor Company's corporate headquarters are in Michigan, and Tyson Foods, the firm that bought up Weaver's Chicken of New Holland, is based in Arizona.

Concurring with Wenger at the same hearing was Pennsylvania State Representative Jere Schuler, who presented the results of a "survey" of 800 voters. Schuler testified that 73 percent of those polled supported a new Route 23 out to Bareville from Lancaster and 69 percent supported extending it out to New Holland.*

Yet when cross-examined, Schuler acknowledged that Amish and Mennonite farmers in the area do not vote and may not have been

---

*Shreiber, Ernest, "Routes 30, 23, 741 Too Narrow, Countians Tell PA." *The Lancaster New Era*, March 15, 1991, pages 1, 8.

included in the poll's mailing list. Tom Baldridge of the Lancaster Chamber of Commerce nonetheless told members of the commission that a new highway was essential for a "vibrant" economy.*

Sitting silently throughout the hearings was Abraham Blank. Blank voiced his concerns several weeks later in an unusually terse article he wrote for an Amish periodical. The piece was titled "When Do We Move?"

Blank wrote, "Occasionally those who have city life education have worked their way to holding offices. . . . They have very little knowledge of the Amish lifestyle and their old traditions. They want to enforce laws that are different from our way of life. The Amish farmer can not in free conscience adapt himself to the laws brought on to them. . . . When is the time to do as our forefathers did years ago, 'Move out of Lancaster County?' "

At the end of Abraham Blank's remarks the publication's editor added his own commentary. "This article is very fitting," he noted. "It carries more weight than any other we had for a long time. All earthly things reach a climax and apparently the Pequea [Valley Amish] settlement has."

Both article and commentary are significant. They are the most direct call to leave Lancaster County by Amish elders I have read. So I mailed a copy of Abraham Blank's article to Governor Casey's office, adding my own editorial: "Notice that this piece is not called "Should We Move?" or "What If We Move?" It's called "*When* Do We Move?"

◆

And so it seems that the push for some sort of superhighway through the Plain People's farmland will continue. Piecemeal, Route 30 will probably be widened over time, from the hamlet of Gap straight into Lancaster, until a highway has crept in almost unnoticed.

In January 1992, the *Lancaster New Era* reported that Ford New Holland was vacating its Franklin Street headquarters in the borough of New Holland and consolidating operations at its Diller Avenue

*Ibid.

48

complex. The move, attributed to recent staff cutbacks by the struggling company, is significant because it weakens Noah Wenger's argument for a new Route 23.

Despite the fact that Commonwealth coffers cannot really support a new superhighway, strident rhetoric espousing its merit continues, while those whose way of life it would disrupt tend their fields and pray on Sunday mornings, singing songs of persecution and faith.

PART EIGHT

I gave them your word, and the world

has hated them for it.

—John 17:14

◆

Tourist Complains to Police about Amish
(*Lancaster Sunday News*, August 21, 1988)

You'd think that with all the media attention the Amish have received over the past several years, most everyone would know at
least a little bit about the Plain People living among their modern
neighbors here.

And yet, some tourists must think this is Williamsburg, where
the scenery is a reconstruction and the costumed inhabitants are
government employees.

Sergeant Richard Zenk of the state police's Lancaster barracks
said he ran into just such a confused tourist, a woman from New
York, last week.

Zenk said the woman came into the barracks Tuesday along with
her husband, saying she wanted to make a complaint against a local
Amishman she had just seen plowing his field along Route 340.
When Zenk asked her why, she reported that the Amish farmer
would not stop to allow her to take a photograph of him standing next
to her husband.

After the visitor had followed the Amishman down the road trying in vain to elicit his cooperation, she decided to take action,
Zenk said.

The woman told Zenk she wanted to report the Amishman to his employer, and wondered if he worked for the county or the state.

Zenk said he had a difficult time stifling his laughter. But he explained to the woman that the man she had seen was an actual member of a religious sect that leads a plain and simple life, and was actually farming his land when the woman accosted him.

"You mean they're not getting paid for this?" the visitor asked with surprise.

"They left shaking their heads, as if they didn't believe it," Zenk said of the tourist and her husband.

◆

Tourist Tells Shocking Story about Lancaster and Amish
(Lancaster Intelligencer Journal, September 8, 1988)

Local farmers will get a charge out of this story.

During a recent visit to Lancaster County, a New York woman decided local officials should pass a law requiring farmers to post warning signs on electric fences, Brenda Brown, of the Lancaster Chamber of Commerce, said today.

Common around rural areas, the fences keep livestock from straying outside the farm grounds.

According to Ms. Brown, the woman pulled off the road last weekend with her son to snap a picture of an Amish youngster. Her son reportedly backed into the fence and got a jolt, which upset the woman. Ms. Brown told her the county has no rules on such matters. The visitor was less than satisfied.

PART NINE

A people has invaded my land, mighty and
without number. —Joel 1:6

◆

September 21, 1988. Harrisburg, PA.

*Pennsylvania Governor Robert P. Casey announces the latest fig-
ures from the U.S. Travel Data Center: spending by tourists visiting
the state is up: almost $11.6 billion dollars in 1987—an increase of
14.8 percent, signifying the first gain in the national tourist market in
eight years. The breakdown of that figure for Lancaster County shows
that tourists spent $71 million more there in 1987 than in 1986, for
a total 1987 figure of $416 million. "This exciting news for Pennsyl-
vania," Casey declares, "speaks loud and clear about the aggressive,
results-oriented approach we've taken to promoting the state's second
largest industry."*

◆

More than 5 million tourists visit Lancaster County annually, thanks
to a $1.5 million yearly advertising campaign by the Pennsylvania
Dutch Visitors' Bureau, the county's umbrella tourism promotional
organization. The Visitors' Bureau had a membership of 400 attractions in 1980. Ten years later the figure stood at over 600.

Harry Flick, current head of the Pennsylvania Dutch Visitors' Bureau, has stated that according to surveys the Visitors' Bureau hands
tourists as they leave the county, outlet store shopping is now rated

the number-one attraction, not Lancaster County's 16,000 Amish. The marketing logic here is flawless: come shop, and while you do, marvel at these antiquated people.

The most recent addition to the Pennsylvania Dutch Visitors' Bureau roster of attractions is a steamboat-shaped inn named for Lancaster County native Robert Fulton. As the final decade of the twentieth century begins, the Amish of Lancaster County, Pennsylvania, have the distinction of being one of America's most popular tourist attractions.

Throughout the county tourists pull their large vehicles off narrow country roads onto steep or sometimes dangerously thin shoulders to take pictures of everything around them: Amish mules working a field; Amish men and boys baling alfalfa; Amish women mowing their neat lawns with push-mowers; Amish wash hanging out to dry on high, angled clotheslines; herds of Holsteins; and each other. Often carloads of tourists pass an Amish carriage while someone literally hangs out the window holding a video camera. Tourists often pull up to a farmhouse in their cars and watch an Amish family go about its business. There is something surreal about dozens of cars parked along rural roads, with those inside staring blankly through camera shutters. Sometimes tourists eagerly jump out and ask if they can "have a look around."

It is all mutually degrading. Neither group is presented to the other realistically. Tourists, given a stern glance or avoided by the Amish, are saddened that their genuine interest or curiosity is met with such severity and conclude that the Amish are cold and unfeeling. The Amish, feeling "like monkeys in a zoo," are offended by tourist picture-taking, which they consider the making of graven images.

The fact is, many of the 600-plus tourist attractions in Lancaster County market mere symbols of what they cannot possess: the Amish way of life, as represented by straw hats, shoo-fly pies, goofy-looking dolls, salt-and-pepper shakers, postcards, T-shirts, and calendars. In promotional material distributed by the Visitors' Bureau to huckster Lancaster County's car museums, bus tours, outlet stores, pretzel factories, and artificial "Amish homesteads," the Amish are exploited as the lure.

But the lure is phony. There really is no medium for genuine exchange between the Amish and English tourists. First of all, the Amish don't really want one: they see themselves as a "peculiar people, a people set apart," enjoined by their faith to remain separate from the world. And second, in terms of sheer numbers, there simply is no way for 5 million tourists on holiday to interact meaningfully with 16,000 Amish hard at work. No transactions are possible beyond the buying and selling of goods at roadside stands or in shops.

But I understand what has brought the tourists. It is the same thing that brought me. After weeks at the Stoltzfus farm I still find myself running to the window to watch a market wagon clip by, glancing into the driver's side—on the right—to see who might be driving.

The picture the Amish of Lancaster County present and what it represents is one of order, symmetry, and calm, of people who have a direct hand in their own affairs, who do their own work, who are responsible for the life around them—and each other. We English come to Lancaster County because we pine for the sanctity the Amish struggle to maintain. As we watch them pass us by we realize all of the values we on "the outside" have long forgone.

Levi Stoltzfus once remarked as we tried to make our way through the mess that is Intercourse mid-day, "In the old days of the Anabaptists in Europe, they were executed in public—for spectacle. Well, like a buddy of mine says, 'This tourism, it's a bloodless theatre!'"

◆

Prophetically, in 1973, an Amish minister wrote a stern editorial in an Amish periodical warning his people about their increased participation in the tourist industry. He likened the arrival of tourism in Lancaster County to a symbol of false promise:

The tourist industry came into our community much like the Trojan Horse. It was a beautiful young animal to behold as it marched up and down Main Street, it brought more trade for the merchants, more ready cash for the banker so the business was promoted and advertised.

With time we did notice that the animal is getting unruly, but none with authority raised a voice against it.

One morning at breakfast, after Levi and Katie, Amos, their thirteen-year-old "hired man," and I milked and fed Levi's thirty-five Holsteins, Elam handed me a book about the history of farming in Lancaster County written by a seventy-four-year-old Amish historian. Elam said, "You might want to read the second-to-last chapter on 'Tourists in Lancaster County.' I think it's pretty true in what's going on here."

So that night I sat reading by the light of a hurricane lamp:

The public officials claim that this tourist business brings to our community more prosperity, millions of dollars are being spent on souvenirs, gas, lodging, eats, etc. But on the other hand, it brings on such problems as already overcrowded highways, the need of building more and better roads, bridges, lodging facilities, motels, restaurants, and gas stations, and brings into our community more industries. More people from our larger cities want to live in our section of the country. For that reason, more homes need to be built, and more families with children mean more schools are needed. Every year, thousands of acres of highly productive land is [sic] being used in building developments, new roads and factories, making the price of farm land more competitive to the extent that the Amish people are being pressed to move to other areas where they can enjoy a more peaceful form of life. . . .

The Amish of today are not intentionally being driven out of this well-established farm community through persecution as our forefathers endured, but because of the great wave of prosperity. [Throughout, the names of Amish sources have been omitted to protect their privacy.]

◆

Lancaster County currently possesses agricultural blessings unlike those found anywhere else in the United States. Its soils are among the richest in the world. Its climate is ideal for a wide variety of produce. Its 5,000 family-owned-and-operated farms produced $575 million worth of dairy products and produce in 1987, more than the farm production of thirteen separate states. And the fact of Lancaster County's incredible proximity to Philadelphia and the megalopolis of the Eastern seaboard adds credence to its reputation as "the Garden Spot of America."

But there is a steadily increasing sprinkling of tract housing on that landscape, much like sprouting weeds in an otherwise immaculate garden. Closer to Lancaster City, the farmland abruptly halts, giving way to monotonous, refuse-strewn steelyards of High Steel Structures and its warehouses, industrial parks, Route 30, and all the city's filthy, backyard debris.

In the summer of 1988 Ed Klimuska, a reporter for the *Lancaster New Era*, wrote a series of articles documenting the destruction of Lancaster County farmland. Klimuska began his series by comparing Lancaster County with Bucks County, Pennsylvania—the latter now a vast landscape of suburban tract housing where farmland once prevailed. He warned:

County leaders brag that Lancaster County's solid economy is built on three pillars: agriculture, business-industry and tourism. . . . This is what the Chamber [of Commerce] wrote in its March report on the County's transportation needs:
"The dramatic growth of this county is attributable to its unique balance among agriculture, industry, and tourism."
That sounds right. But it's wrong. This is reality: The county's 'unique balance' broke down in the past decade. Business and industry soared. Tourism fattened. But farming declined. The breakdown is altering the county's landscape, revising its economic structure, and threatening to turn an American farming oasis into a Bucks County West.*

Reflecting these trends, Lancaster County's employment growth was 18.1 percent for the period 1983—87, compared to 9 percent for the rest of Pennsylvania and 11.5 percent for the United States.

The Amish are not free of implication in this alarming transition: the boom has also brought prosperity to them. It has been estimated that 50 percent of the Amishmen living in Lancaster County now make their living away from the family farm, in thriving small shops of all kinds, or on construction crews. In the early morning it is common to see van loads of Amishmen being driven by English drivers to construction sites throughout the county, making a wage they could never earn on the family farm. In addition, wooden lawn-furniture manufacturers, quilt shops, repair shops, paint stores, and storage-barn manufacturers now dot the Amish countryside.

Two hundred Amishmen who wanted to farm in 1988 were unable

* Klimuska, Ed, "Lancaster County: The (Ex?) Garden Spot of America," Lancaster, Pa.: *The Lancaster New Era*, Reprint, July 1988.

to do so because there were no farms for them. Amish family farms have been subdivided again and again to accommodate a population that has doubled in the past twenty years and there is no more room. For the first time in its history the 250-year continuity of Amish family life has been interrupted. Farming as a mainstay of the Lancaster County Amish is rapidly coming to an end. Half the Amish living in the County today are under the age of eighteen, and the question of how this entire generation of Amish will earn its livelihood hovers ominously in the air. Pondering it, one Amish bishop noted, "The lunch pail is the greatest threat to our way of life." *

◆

In an introduction to an Amish Directory published in 1989, its editor wondered, "If another directory was to be made, what would it look like? We are near a very critical stage of time in Lancaster County, concerning the Amish Church."

He then reflected on where his people have been and where they seem to be heading, given his compiled statistics for the Directory:

When our fathers implanted our church in Lancaster County it was their will, even a part of their faith, to live on a farm to raise their family, to live together and work together. The immigrant Stoltzfus family was the back-bone of the establishment of our community here. They had an unwritten motto to live together, worship together, stay together, and die together. That cohesiveness is one fundamental that built our churches to what they are today and certainly was an instrument in building our county to the state of being named "The Garden Spot of the World." Until 1940 very few Amish heads [of families] were employed in off-farm jobs. By 1960 this practice rose and we began to realize the squeeze of available farmland diminishing and a fast-growing population. The conservative families that could not farm took to building and operating repair shops—to repair farm implements, harnesses, buggy shops (and more) which were farm related, needed by the commonwealth of the church and relieved the growing pressure. It was a good second best and still is. These shops were often built on or near the home premises where the family could work together in harmony.

* Kraybill, Donald, *The Riddle of Amish Culture*, Baltimore, Md.: Johns Hopkins University Press, 1989, page 192.

Conditions in the so-called "Garden Spot" today are incredible. With the tourist trade and its industry plus other industry and development all around us, these conditions have lured our people to employment unthought of twenty years ago. We are reluctant to release today's statistics, but without pointing our finger to accuse anyone, we must face the facts: *There are over 100 Amish construction crews in Lancaster County, some travel as far as Delaware and perhaps farther in-state to work in developments that destroy farmland.* There are about the same number of woodwork shops of which many cater to the tourist trade. We have many shops that restore carriages and related items that are pleasing to the world fashion today.

Another editorial about tourism would appear in the October 1989 issue of an Amish publication. After chronicling the county-wide trend "to promote more industry, more development," the author stopped, reminding both himself and his people, "That is the outside world's business, so let's let the rest of the world go by and be concerned about the inside core." Pondering the thought that "God may have sent the tourists into our community as a test to our faith," the author admonished his readers, saying: "If they *were* sent here for that cause, no one with a plain garb should be involved in anything, operate anything, or even promote man-made attractions to the tourists. That would be openly showing denial to our faith."

He then traced the roots of increased "open denial" among the Amish and their obliviousness to the trend: "Twenty years ago there were columns written in a newspaper that the tourist industry is reaping great profits at the expense of the Amish. In the last ten years this trend has reversed: *Many 'plain people' are now profiting from the tourist.*

"It is surprising that so little is talked about it among our people. What we hear comes from liberal groups saying things as: 'Oh we never had it so good. Our church districts are growing at an all-time high rate, we are prospering. What a blessing!' The more conservative or concerned people will say: 'We are living in the latter days of time,' which is definitely the whole truth."

The author warned of the devastation that would result from being "of the world," by interpreting Luke 17:32:

Lot had the same heritage as Abraham. And Lot also had flocks and herds and herdsmen. When the time came that they must part, Lot chose the

Plain of Jordan 'that it was well-watered, even as the Garden of the Lord.' In its time certainly it was the Garden Spot of the World. While Scripture is silent for a period of time about their livelihood there, we assume that they fared well in the garden, herding cattle and sheep, living in tents, with contentment. After a while the city of Sodom perhaps industrialized and developed into the garden. In another while Lot was found to live in the city with his family. The angels were commanded to warn Lot of the vile state of Sodom—that it will be destroyed with fire and brimstones. After the angels led Lot and his wife away from destruction, they were commanded to retreat to the mount, and not to look back. Lot got his wife out of the city, but he never got Sodom out of his wife, so she disobeyed, looked back, and now stands as a statue.

Perhaps our Lord uses this allusion that we should remember this statue as a memorial and portrait—to see her with dropped head and sinister eyes gazing at a place which was once a wondrous garden that is now a replica of destruction.

◆

To be Amish in Lancaster County, Pennsylvania, means to face trial—not from religious or governmental edict, but rather from short-term prosperity and county-wide bureaucratic oblivion. Increasingly surrounded by suburbanization and commercialism, the Amish struggle to honor the central exhortation of the Old Order Amish Church—avoidance of conformity with the world. The struggle of the Amish against "worldy conformity" takes a particular form in Lancaster County—economic reliance on the "outside" versus self-sufficiency.

To be a farmer who earns his primary livelihood on a construction crew building tract houses, to be a waitress in a restaurant or a clerk in a store, to hang a sign outside one's farm along busy Route 340 advertising the sale of quilts or wooden lawn furniture is to be "yoked" to the outside world and fundamentally at odds with the Amish faith.

"Soon there'll be two Amish groups here," Elam mused one Sunday afternoon as he put away his German Bible. "There'll be farmers and the trade people. And that will be the end of us," he said.

Increasing economic change from without threatens Amish cohesion from within. The Ordnung, an unwritten set of Amish church mores, attempts to "hold the line" for the community of believers. Of that attempt, and the congregation's response to it, an Amish minister has written: "Our church fathers had a strong desire to hold on to the old way of life, and although much has changed over the years, they have been successful in 'holding the line' to the point that we have been separated from the world. This did not come overnight. . . .

"Obedience is a close associate of Ordnung [which, roughly translated, means 'discipline' or 'order']. It signals whether you love the church or if you do not. You are either in the church or you are outside. There is no happy medium."

"You are either in the church or you are outside" is a statement Elam also uses often, in sermons to his people at church and day after day as we drive through the county.

"We're living in the final days, but our people just don't see it," Elam sighs. It is his people's blindness that worries Elam Stoltzfus the most.

◆

When the Amish speak English rather than Dutch in my presence I have sometimes heard talk about "scouting parties"—groups of Amishmen quietly looking over land in other parts of the country. When the *Lancaster Sunday News* ran a front-page story in March 1989 about Amish scouting parties, Elam and Levi read it with great interest. The article stated that, given current trends in Lancaster County "options [by Amish] on at least one large parcel of land, about 4,000 acres in Kentucky, have reportedly been taken and further trips are anticipated." * This was confirmation for many English of what had been rumored for months: some Amish are preparing to move out.

"Well, I'll be," Elam exclaims, "I knew about our boys visiting Ohio, but Kentucky! That's news to me!"

One Sunday evening in the kitchen Levi Stoltzfus ponders his children's future while Benuel and Rebecca play nearby. "I see it

*Thomas, Doug, "Greener Pastures for the Amish?" *Lancaster Sunday News*, March 5, 1989, page 1.

going like this," he begins. "With all the building going on here, soon our people will start moving out, for places like Kentucky. The Amish who stay will be the ones who have big profitable businesses. After a time, they'll leave the church, or start driving cars and using electricity. It's like it says in the book my father gave you to read, 'Prosperity has often been fatal to Christianity, but persecution, never.'"

In late July, Elam Stoltzfus asks me to drive him to Cecil County, Maryland, just on the other side of the Pennsylvania/Maryland border—an area noted for its productive farmland. Once there, we drive around and around. I kid Elam saying, "Now you and I are just like the tourists in Lancaster County." But the joke falls on deaf ears; this is no afternoon in the country for Elam Stoltzfus. He looks urgently at the passing countryside.

"Pull over," he says suddenly. Elam gets out and feels the earth between his fingers. The temperature is in the high 90s. The wind provides no relief. The earth is dry and becomes powdery when Elam crumbles it, and the corn is droopy—not at all like the tall, straight corn standing in Stoltzfus's fields back home. He walks down a row of corn with his arms outstretched and his fingers spread wide, feeling it like a cat with its whiskers. The wind blows his long white beard. He stands in the middle of the row for a long time, very still. I think of Lear on the heath. Finally he gets back into the car. "Well," Elam sighs, "I just wanted to see this land down here. I had to get it out of my system. We might as well go on home."

A people has invaded my land,
mighty and without number;
His teeth are the teeth of a lion,
and his molars those of a lioness.
He has laid waste my vine,
and blighted my fig tree;
He has stripped it, sheared off its bark;
its branches are made white. . . .
Alas, the day!
for near is the day of the Lord,
and it comes as ruin from the Almighty.
From before our very eyes
has not the food been cut off;
And from the house of our God,
Joy and gladness?
The seed lies shriveled under its clods;
the stores are destroyed,
The barns are broken down,
for the grain has failed.
How the beasts groan!
The herds of cattle are bewildered!
Because they have no pasturage.
Even the flocks of sheep have perished.
To you, O Lord, I cry!
for fire has devoured the pastures
of the plain,
and flame has enkindled all the trees
of the field.
—Joel 1:6–7; 15–19

◆

To you, O Lord, I cry!

A people has invaded Lancaster County. Mighty and without number. Shiftless and without root, seeking root. Their souls have been invaded. Sanctity has left them, so they destroy what is sanctified over generations.

Their teeth are the legal teeth of the lawyer, their molars those of the politician, that grind the lowly to a pulp, that wear them away with hearing after hearing and destroy the faith in their souls.

They have laid waste the vine and blighted the corn field. They have stripped it, sheared away its abundance for apartments and factories.

Alas the day!

For near is the day of the Lord, and it comes as ruin from the Almighty. From before our very eyes, has not the food been cut off?

And from the house of our God, joy and gladness?

The seed lies shriveled under concrete, the stores have been built by people far, far away.

The old barns are broken down and destroyed, for the grain has failed. How the beasts groan!

The herds of cattle are bewildered! They are crowded off their pasturage, which is turned to stores. Even the flocks of sheep have perished.

To you, O Lord, I cry!

The streams of water are dried up, and flame devours sanctity in a comely people.

The flame of greed, shame, and rage.

The blaze of lost faith.

The suffocation of progress.

The pitch of boredom.

The flares of indifference.

The conflagration of growth.

The annihilation of harassment.

The burning legal fury of vengeance as knowledge.

To you, O Lord, I cry!

For fire devours the pastures of the Plain.

And flame enkindles the wracks of their farms.

PART TEN

After the fire there was a tiny whispering
sound.   —1 Kings 19:12

◆

Paradise, PA. 3:15 A.M.

*Screaming sirens pierce the black country night. In the sky to the
south of the Stoltzfus farm a bright orange glow shoots through the
stillness, while the voices of shouting men dissipate like vapor across
acres of just-sprouting corn.*

*Rachel gets out of bed in her white long-sleeved nightshirt and
stocking cap to open and close the windows at least three times. She
plods down the creaky stairs and heads into the kitchen to look out
the windows facing east. The sirens have me dreaming I am back in
Boston. Shorty goes up and down the wooden stairs to the kitchen, his
pointy toenails clicking on the kitchen's linoleum floor. He jumps up
on the table, looking out the window whenever Rachel does likewise.
Normally Rachel would scold him in Dutch and swat him down off the
table. But tonight she lets him see the red sky too. Across the Belmont
Road, in the middle of Aaron Lapp's pasture, a lone heifer stands
bawling on a hill—long, high, grunting moos, her neck upstretched
like a coyote's.*

It is a torn-up night, the third act of Chekhov's Three Sisters.
Through it all, Elam snores soundly. . . .

◆

In the check-out line at Zimmerman's Store the next morning, at Kauffman's Produce on the way to Smoketown, at roadside stands selling shoo-fly pies and wooden lawn furniture, the talk among the Amish is all the same.

Elam, Levi, and I find out by driving in the direction Rachel, Levi, and I first saw orange sky. When we see two Amishmen working in a lumber yard near Route 30, Elam says, "Pull over." He gets out and returns a minute later. He gets in the Horizon, slams the door, turns to Levi and says, "LeRoy Blank's."

That night at supper, Rachel says, "Why, uh, they're gonna need help with the clean-up at LeRoy's. Elam can't go, he's too old, and Levi has milking, but he sent his hired man, Amos. You might want to go along too. It might be interesting to you."

In some sense, the suggestion is also a challenge. For Rachel in particular—much the shrewder judge of character than Elam—this is another way to find out who I am. For the Amish, being known and knowing others constitutes the heart of community. Thus the suggestion to go help out is an important step, one not taken lightly or offered willy nilly.

So I put on faded blue jeans, a work shirt, jean jacket and L.L. Bean boots and head over to LeRoy Blank's in the Horizon, frightened but intrigued.

LeRoy Blank is an ex-Amish egg farmer. His long rectangular barn sits perpendicular to a gravel lane that veers into his property. One end of the barn is burnt clear through, owing to a short in the electrical wiring system used to keep the chickens warm.

When I drive over at about six, dozens of people are already helping out—mostly Old Order Amishmen and boys. Women and girls are bringing food and drink back and forth from the farmhouse. On first sight, this looks like an Amish "frolic." I ask a short man in a navy-blue jumpsuit, "Can you use an extra hand?"

"Sure, just climb that ladder and you can help haul out chickens," he says.

I slosh through mud caused by fire hoses aimed at the barn all night. I go through the doorway and my foot disappears into two feet of chicken manure. The smell is acrid beyond description. I pull my foot out cursing, and the man I first spoke to yells, "No! *Next* door!"

An aluminum ladder leans against the opposite end of the barn. I climb it. Entering the barn is like jumping off a high dive, straight into blackness. I follow an Amishman in a navy-blue denim coat. At the top of the ladder are about ten long rows of stacked chicken coops. Between the rows are narrow lanes, like catwalks in the highest spaces of a theater. Men and boys are walking back and forth along them.

Those walking away from the burned end of the barn hold fistfuls of dead white chickens bunched together at the feet. Those walking into the darkness go to fetch more dead chickens. The dead birds are pitched out open barn doors into a giant lime-green dumpster below. There is something unnerving about its cheerful color.

For the first few minutes it is so dark I feel like a blind man. You walk down the catwalk, turning to your side when somebody meets you with arms loaded down with dead chickens, they doing likewise—a macabre tango step. You maneuver around each other, they heading toward the light of the opened, second-story doors, you plunging into darkness and the smell of singed flesh.

Eerie, erratic flashlight beams. Black figures in straw hats riffling through the coops, finding dead chickens, yanking them out. The sound of tearing flesh and feathers, the dulled moaning of the birds still alive, the whole upstairs of the barn sounding like a nursery for the insane, as if children who have shrieked all night now have no more voice so they moan quietly and softly and slowly.

For a moment I think I am in the classroom of my nightmares. The smell of smoke makes me sit down. The walls contract. An Amishman asks quietly, "Are you poorly?" Amish boys spit in the cracks between the catwalk boards. An English teenager says, "I feel like a mercenary." I feel my heart pounding, then say, "I'm fine, but thank you."

After a moment, I am surprisingly calm, perhaps because everyone else is. Many are here to pitch in; it seems amazing to have so much help for so disturbing a job.

I put my hand right up to the large, calloused hand of an Amishman yanking birds from the coops. He hands me a leg. I find myself playing with it while waiting to be handed more dead chickens, surprised that death feels fleshy and bony, like an old lady's fingers.

I literally bump into Amos King, Levi and Katie's "hired man," and am relieved to find him here. Thirteen, a string bean with yellow hair and wide blue eyes, Amos is a strong, quiet presence. As Rachel and I watched him walk down the lane one day, Rachel remarked, "See how that boy walks? He has ambition in him."

In a way, it's a quiet business. People don't talk much, out of a kind of respect. They are handed chickens, they walk down the catwalks to the opened upper-floor doors and pitch the chickens, which land like little white pillows. I throw some and watch them land. There is a boy of about eighteen, very muscular, shirtless, walking up and down for some of the Mennonite girls on hand below.

At eight o'clock in the evening, Amos and I leave. The sky is purple, like a Santa Fe sky. Long wafts of clouds are golden at their edges. We climb down the aluminum ladder and walk down the lane, along a just-plowed cornfield, to the Horizon sitting next to a line of buggies.

"I'm glad we're going home, aren't you, Amos?" I ask.

"Yep!" he says with his broad smile.

"And I'm not eating chicken for a long time," I add.

"That's about right!" Amos laughs.

At the Stoltzfus's the sitting room is lit by two hurricane lamps. Rachel sits crocheting a white doily in her willow rocker, talking to an old, short Amishman with a huge overhanging brow whose name is Joe. He is a cousin of Elam's. Elam is asleep in the next room; his breaths are short and deep. He almost snores.

"P-U! You smell like *chickens*!" Rachel says the minute I come up from the basement entryway. Then after a pause she asks, "Well? How was it?" I recount the whole affair while Rachel rocks and stitches and Elam's cousin Joe listens with his gray eyes reflecting the golden, kerosene light. The chimes from the upstairs bedroom strike nine. "There's water heated up for a bath if you want to take one," Rachel says.

I hang up my clothes, which reek of manure and death. It will take three days for them to air out. I pour water heated on the basement stove into the bathtub with a shiny chrome bucket, and barely get into bed before I am lost to sleep, dreaming for the last time about my classroom, and about the one live chicken I saw in the lime-green dumpster, surrounded by death, and the muscular boy with no shirt who spotted it, fetched a big rock, and bashed in its head until it too was dead—in a shocking way, an act of grace.

◆

LeRoy Blank's barn fire has implications for the larger Amish community not readily discernible to an outsider.

"You have to be able to count on your neighbors. That's an important part of being Amish," Levi Stoltzfus says as we stop at LeRoy Blank's a few weeks after the fire to see how rebuilding is going. "And not just at frolics. It means during bad times too. Maybe more so then."

"See, LeRoy used to be Amish," Rachel adds after LeRoy Blank stops by several weeks later to see Elam. "He left twenty years ago. He joined a liberal church, started driving a truck and got his house hooked up with electricity. His minister, well first he had a car, then a bigger car, then an AIRPLANE! But then LeRoy saw what it was doing to his boys. And then this fire. Electricity. LeRoy thinks it's a sign. People hope he's on his way back to the church. That's why so many turned out to help with cleanup. LeRoy's done the hardest part—asking to come back. Still, it'll be hard to face the community. But now the community will be tested. LeRoy's test is over. It will be up to them to accept him."

In August I drive Elam over to LeRoy Blank's. The barn is repaired. The two have a good visit while I sit in the Horizon for almost an hour. It is unlike Elam to keep anyone waiting, or not to invite me in whenever he goes in an Amish home.

But today is different.

Elam is counseling LeRoy about "the way back." He comes out of the house saying little. Several weeks later, LeRoy and his family get on their knees before the local Amish church district "to beg forgiveness" as Rachel calls it—an emotional ordeal for both penitents and congregation. Within days after coming back, LeRoy Blank sells his truck, rips out the electrical wiring in the house and barn, and dons Amish clothing once again.

After the Blanks rejoin the church, there is a tiny whispering sound throughout the Amish community—muted though joyous acknowledgment. The community has passed the test.

PART ELEVEN

The fields are shining for harvest!

—John 4:35

◆

Across Lancaster County everyone is baling alfalfa, and everyone is baling it in exactly the same way. Standing on the highest bale in the farthest field of the Stoltzfus farm, I count four somber processionals doing exactly what we are doing: Amishmen and boys toward the Welsh Mountains and way out to the Gap, haywagons stacked high with bales of alfalfa behind red and yellow New Holland balers, haywagons now resembling pyramids on wheels pulled by diligent teams of mules. Full wagons are unloaded in suffocatingly hot barns. Empty wagons return to fields. Snorting and sweating, the teams step carefully. Around and around the fields, mules step and sweat, driven by callused hands holding leather reins. All day long and into dusk. Unified rhythm. Boys and haywagons. Men and mules. Man and earth. Community at work.

Today Elam stands straight on a forecart, pulling a rake that gathers the cut alfalfa into neat winding rows, long oval rings that circle the field. Rarely using the seat behind him, Elam is the picture of dignity, back straight in white shirt with sleeves rolled up, every now and then spitting tobacco juice over his shoulder, pulling on the reins, guiding the mules with an occasional command.

Levi drives a team of four mules that pull a New Holland baler he bought used from an Amish horse trader in Goshen. It scoops up the hay Elam has raked and packs it into rectangular blocks that it binds with two pieces of baling twine. Then it spits the bales down a chute, one at a time toward the haywagon, which is hitched directly behind it. Standing on the haywagon I yank the bales off the chute and lug them to Amos. He is at the rear of the wagon, stacking them, until the bales form a perfect pyramid.

The baler lumbers along in a flattened whir. Exhaust mixed with flecks of chaff straw blows into our eyes as we stand on the wagon. Amos has a monkey ring around his lips from licking them constantly as we bale. Katie, Rebecca, and Benuel bring out water and mint tea (made with mint yanked by Rebecca from the nearby meadow) in plastic gallon milk containers every time we haul in a load of hay. A red plastic thermos filled with ice water hangs from a nail on the back slats of the haywagon. We drink constantly.

After one load is gathered, I run to the Horizon and turn on the radio to know just how hot it is: the country-western radio station from Ephrata reports it is 94 degrees, and the humidity is nearly 100 percent.

Everything and everyone comes together during baling. Elam and Levi work side by side. Katie and Rachel take turns bringing drinks into the fields. On days when Amos must go home early to his own family, Katie drives the team of mules pulling the baler while Levi jumps on the haywagon and loads. (In fact, it is Katie who teaches me how to drive a sprayer across the alfalfa, using the wheel marks from the previous pass to guide the next.) In a pinch, Aaron Lapp will lend Levi his haywagon or Levi and Amos will cross the Belmont Road and help Aaron bring in a few loads.

It is rhythm we seek. Rhythm is the pattern of community. Today we have found it.

RRrruumm-RRrruumm; RRrruumm-RRrruumm. RRrruumm-RRrruumm; RRrruumm-RRrruumm. RRrruumm-RRrruumm; RRrruumm-RRrruumm. RRrruumm-RRrruumm; RRrruumm-RRrruumm. RRrruumm-RRrruumm.

To me it is extraordinary to think that this, like morning milking, is going on everywhere around us. For the Amish, though, it is an ordinary part of community life. Maybe this is what is meant by being separate from the world—that what is done as a matter of course *within* the community is regarded as a curiousity from *without*. I think of tourists lined up along Route 340 in July, taking pictures from the porch of a hotel across the highway of Benuel Smoker as he and his boys bale their fields.

Precisely who declares the alfalfa "fit to bale" is hard to say. Farming is a constant matter of prediction, anticipation, and assessment. Elam and Levi check the mule-shaped weathervane on top of their white wooden-and-stone barn. Elam watches the clouds constantly, all summer long. He will worry about the weather until the heavy rains come in late July.

On a trip to southern Lancaster County to look at a crimper Elam wants to buy for Levi's birthday, we stop at an old gas station. "Are you folks having as dry a summer down here as we are farther up?" Elam asks smiling.

Like one of Flannery O'Connor's rural characters, the old gas station attendant hitches up his blue coveralls, spits into the dust, leans right into the car, and says in an undertone, "Well you know what they say. 'Dry June means a dry summer.' "

"Yeah, I guess you're right," Elam says thinly, again trying to smile. But I can see that he regards the attendant as prophetic.

Once we're back on the road, Elam is silent for a time. Then he turns to me and says, "I kinda wish that man hadn't a said what he did. The way he said it makes me think he's right. That won't be good for the farmer, I'm afraid."

The weather in Lancaster County is a force, a presence, something to know and watch, a shaper, a decider—almost a being. Drought will wither the county's corn and turn the alfalfa into deadened grass. An ill-timed rain, once Levi has cut his alfalfa, can be equally destructive. It might make the alfalfa moldy. "Cows won't touch it if we try and feed it to them," Levi remarks while watching the sky. "A lot of what it takes to be a good farmer is knowing how to second-guess the weather."

Can the alfalfa be cut, left to dry, and baled before the rains come? Are the thunderheads moving along the Welsh Mountains? Is the air heavy? Levi and Elam consult constantly throughout the entire process of cutting, raking, and baling. Once the hay's cut, Levi and Elam walk each morning after breakfast to the edge of the garden nearest the house and then into the hayfield. Then Elam

gathers a handful of alfalfa and sifts it through his wide hands to judge whether it is sufficiently dry.

But everyone knows when it is time to bale. And everyone acts accordingly. When the first man in the Meadowbrook church district—the Stoltzfus's district—sets out to bale, the rest quickly follow suit. Nobody wants to be last to haul in his alfalfa.

As Elam, Levi, Amos, and I push to finish the upper field late in the afternoon, Rachel drives Pat and the market wagon up the Belmont Road (with Benuel and Rebecca along), turns up the embankment, and goes straight across the field. Levi shuts down the baler and the whirring stops. He stands watching his mother as she drives Pat toward us, buggy springs creaking.

Seeing the buggy, Elam stops raking and says, "Relief!"

"Who's hungry?!" Rachel yells like Annie Oakley. She climbs out of the market wagon and passes out sloppy joes on weiner buns, a thermos of ice water, vanilla sandwich cookies, two mayonnaise jars full of "lemon" for Elam—concentrated lemonade made with less water than called for, according to Elam's taste—and a mayonnaise jar filled with chocolate milk for Levi, *his* passion. Elam guzzles the lemon. Rebecca jumps out of the buggy and hands him a blanket. He climbs under the haywagon, spreads the blanket and lies down on it, resting in the shade for a minute. He puts his straw hat over his face. Sprawled on the ground now, Elam looks old and tired, like a knocked-over scarecrow.

The mules are panting. I can see their sides heaving; their coats are much darker under the harness straps. Sweat. The corn is now over six feet high.

Katie comes down the Belmont Road with an empty haywagon pulled by two fresh mules. She stands on the front of the haywagon as if it were a chariot. Before she turns up the embankment Katie stops traffic with one wide motion of her hand. Her self-assurance is dazzling.

The break is short. Rachel gathers up the containers and climbs back into the buggy. Rebecca and Benuel jump in, Rachel yells, "Go on, Pat!"

And then they are gone.

The buggy heads diagonally across the field, a wide trail of dust in its wake. Katie drives back with the tired mules and a full load of baled alfalfa.

The next load we do is "early hay," green so that each bale is heavy. While Levi goes to lend Aaron Lapp a hand, he asks Amos if he would drive the team and loaded-up haywagon back to the barn. There Amos and I will unload it.

Along the fields are dirt roads running parallel to the Belmont Road. I jump off the haywagon at the crest of the hill to signal for the traffic to slow while Amos, standing on the front of the wagon, takes the team down off the field lane and onto the Belmont Road, at a snail's pace. He is headed for a leveled place across the road where he can bring the team safely up the embankment without spilling the hay. But while I am watching for traffic, Amos misses the spot. The haywagon tips its load right onto the Belmont Road with tourist traffic racing straight toward us at fifty miles an hour.

Levi, Aaron Lapp, and his youngest son come running from Aaron's fields. All of us pitch the bales onto the shoulder of the road in less than a minute: Levi and Aaron taking the bales by twos; Amos, Aaron's son, and I one at a time. This is all done in absolute silence. No blame is laid. The event itself is sufficient lesson.

Later, an empty haywagon sits in the middle of the upper field. Amos has gone home to help his own family prepare for Sunday church. Levi says, "Take the team back to the wagon and hitch them up to it. Then bring the wagon to Pop."

By now I am driving the mules too. But this hasn't come easily. The mules know who can drive them and who can't. For Levi and Elam they work tirelessly, their ears forward as if trying to impress with their stamina. For me, an outsider, their ears go straight back; they sometimes refuse to move, or move when I haven't given a command.

One afternoon the mules decided to back up as I tried to adjust a metal pin which joined the wagon to the end of the tongue. My hand was almost smashed. Furious, I walked to the front of the team, grabbed the lead mule's reins, threw my baseball cap on the ground, and cursed at the top of my lungs for five minutes. Then I gave the order to back up in a voice hard and throaty like Levi's when he orders the cows to get going in Dutch. And the mules backed up!

The pin slid into place. The team and the wagon were hitched together. I got on the wagon to drive it out to Elam. When I looked up, though, I saw Levi and Elam stopped in the middle of the field with their fists on their hips. They had been watching the entire time and they were laughing their heads off.

Later that day Levi nudged me in the ribs and said, "I notice you got the wagon hitched. It's kinda hard to make those mules back up."

Levi and I are taking it easy, sitting on the highest bales of the wagon while Elam drives the team. This is to be the last load of alfalfa for the day.

But Elam is driving right for a huge sinkhole in the middle of the field, oblivious. The baler, mules, and Elam, standing on the forecart, miss the sinkhole, but the right front wheel of the haywagon hits it with a tremendous KA-THUD!

The haywagon dips.

I grab Levi.

We look at each other wide-eyed. In a matter of seconds the rear wheel will hit too.

"Ho! HO! Pop! POP! HOOOOOOOO!" Levi yells.

But Elam doesn't hear, and now the right rear wheel goes into the hole and the load tips with a slow lean like a torpedoed ship keeling over and we are hurled fifteen feet off the wagon, bales flying everywhere. Still Elam continues driving the team on. Levi runs in front of the team and waves his hands over his head and the mules stop instantly. Then he yells to his father in Dutch.

We quickly reload the wagon with the bales that have fallen off, panting, sweating, anxious to finish. Now the load is seven bales high, not the usual four or five. There isn't any symmetry to the stack. We lug it in as quickly as we can. I am standing high on the top bale. The sides of the stacked hay are wobbly from the spill. God knows how, but we bring it all in.

I help with choring since Amos has gone for the day. As I throw silage thirty feet down from inside the silo with a pitchfork, the air is close, sweet, and humid. I'm sweating and cranky, feeling as if I have been kicked by a cow. So after chores and supper on the picnic table outside I announce, "Well I guess I'll go on in."

Rachel gives me a withering look. "Before the hay's all in?"

"I think we're going to put it in on Monday," I say with absolute authority.

Another Rachel Stoltzfus death stare: an Amish farmer NEVER leaves hay outside over Sunday. It is all put away Saturday night so the fields are empty and the barn is clean for the Sabbath.

I look at Levi and say, "Well, you want to put the hay in?"

"Only if you're up for it," he says, deferring as the Amish always will.

This is another test.

"Let's do it," I say through clenched teeth.

Elam and Levi talk the entire time we are unloading the wagons in the barn about whether the hay was ready to be cut, even as we are putting it away, and about whether the alfalfa stems really do stand up and dry better with the new rake, and whether a drying spray applied to the alfalfa did any good. Elam thinks it made all the difference in the world, and Levi is still undecided. I'm pooped, and I think, "We have been at work today for over fifteen hours. Enough is enough."

Then Elam goes in and Levi and I finish unloading the two hay-wagons. At 8:20 P.M. Levi says, "I want to thank you for your help today. You really kept up, right until the last job."

I am softened, grateful. "Well, coming from you, that means an awful lot." Pause. "But you know what I'd *really* like right now?" I ask. "A BEER!" Levi laughs heartily and we head inside.

On her side of the house Rachel sits eating an ice cream float. When I walk in she gets up and makes me one. Elam is asleep on the couch, a dish of melty chocolate ice cream nearby, Shorty lying on his stomach. I bring two floats over to Katie and Levi's side of the house. By the light of a lantern Rachel has lit in the basement I take a hot bath, falling asleep naked in the white metal tub.

PART TWELVE

That they may be one . . .

—John 17:21

◆

On Saturdays during July (when there is no alfalfa to bale), a light-heartedness descends upon Lancaster County that shatters the image of the Amish as dour. Buggies rumble by just after choring time loaded down with family, picnic baskets, Tupperware containers, shopping bags, fishing rods, baseball mitts, and aluminum lawn chairs. Vanloads of Amish families driven by English drivers race from one end of the county to the other.

It is family reunion season.

Today there is to be one on Rachel's side of the family, the Smuckers, pronounced "Schmookah." Down the Belmont Road I count at least twenty Amishmen, women, and children walking barefoot to family reunions, oblivious to the tour buses slowing to watch.

Rachel has long gone to the reunion, picked up by two of her daughters' families traveling by van. Elam has spent the entire week telling Rachel he won't go to the reunion because he has too much work to do. But now, that is precisely where we are headed. This is great fun for Elam and Rachel. It is the game they play—what the Amish mean when they say "learning how to bend."

We drive down road after road that cuts through cornfields. Occasionally there is wheat, stacked in neat sheaves. Elam says, "There was a time when there was as much wheat grown here as corn you see now. But it doesn't hardly pay for a farmer to grow wheat anymore." It seems ironic that the nation's two long-standing symbols of bounty—the buffalo and wheat sheaves—have outlived their plenitude. On Fourth-of-July weekend I had helped one of Elam's sons, Jacob, harvest wheat on his farm near Strasburg. I worked as hard as I have in my entire life. Looking at the sheaves now, I am aware of how much work is represented by their symmetry.

We drive down Lime Quarry Road. The Smucker farm sits where the road turns past the Limeville Quarry (which is cut from the middle of a cornfield—but seems orderly, as if the quarry and farm have always coexisted, respectful). The farmhouse and two barns make a kind of courtyard. One barn is closer to the road.

There must be over four hundred Amish gathered in the courtyard area. Perhaps thirty carriages are lined up on one side of a field. Farther down the road adolescent boys are playing baseball, with about thirty younger boys, some wearing their black felt hats, watching. A small group of girls watches in the shade of a large tree.

Elam and I walk down the lane to the far barn. Groups of people sit in aluminum lawn chairs. Elam breezes through saying, "Hello, Sam. Hi, Amos. How are you, Isaac?" People think I am a relation so my hand is shaken too. "Are you from the colony in New York?" a woman asks me.

"Nope," I reply, "not me." (How to explain with a quick, polite answer that I am writing a dissertation on what it means to be in the world but not of it?) One of Elam's sons-in-law tells us that Rachel is in the barn.

The barn is dark, cool, and shaded. There are long rows of picnic tables, some bare, some spread with white tablecloths. Families sit in congregations. Some families have finished eating and have turned their chairs inward to form circles. Across from where Elam and I find Rachel is a group of women, some Amish, some Mennonite, speaking Dutch, passing a baby girl in booties around the admiring circle. There is much fussing.

In another corner are three men and their wives in their mid-twenties, all dressed like outsiders—the children of Rachel's one brother who left the church decades ago. They have come in two cars—a red Pontiac convertible and a souped-up pickup truck—parked at the end of the long row of buggies. The pick-up truck reads SMUCKER CONSTRUCTION COMPANY: LANCASTER. The contrast is marked, one I will see sprinkled throughout the uniformity of the Amish gathering today: a circle of thirty Amish in lawn chairs, and a man and woman, also part of the circle, dressed in casual summer "worldly dress"—sons or daughters who elected not to be baptized into the Amish faith. It is stunning to look at a woman of twenty-five in a muslin summer dress and sandals surrounded by her Amish sisters in brown and black.

Elam will explain to me that "in Lancaster County the Amish hold onto about 80 percent of their young people. That's pretty good considering how surrounded we are by temptation." A newly married Amishman from Quarryville will tell me about working on an English construction crew—and of the temptations he felt while doing so. After describing the battle he waged over "staying or leaving" he decided to stay because "in our way of living it's easier to be good. You know where the lines are drawn."

For the most part, those still inside the barn are older people. Rachel helps us fill up our plates. Then she says, "The candy scramble is about to start. Do you want to go watch?" I nod, and Rachel steps ahead, leading the way to the courtyard amidst cries in English and Dutch of "Hello, Aunt Rachel! Hi, Aunt Rachel!"

We are intentionally not walking together. It would be considered improper, Rachel will explain that night, half apologizing, for a married Amish woman to be escorted by an English bachelor in a public gathering. (Rachel and I will not ride alone together in the Horizon until she and I know each other *well*.) The same short woman with gray hair in a brown dress who asked if I was from New York approaches again and asks Rachel in Dutch, "And who's this?"

Rachel has her "I'm-mad-that-you're-being-so-nosy-but-I'll-still-be-nice-to-you" smile on. She replies in English, to clue me in on what's going on, "This is Elam's driver, Randy." Rachel and I keep walking. Rachel has no intention of getting into a discussion about what I'm doing here. I'm relieved for this.

The candy scramble is about forty children—all Amish with the exception of two little boys in crew cuts and shorts and 1950s-style striped polo shirts—holding hands in a wide circle. To me it symbolizes the continuity of the Amish community. A huge circle of joined hands. Behind the children are parents—helpers—bent over, pointing, whispering words of advice, helping to keep the itchy line still. An Amish woman of about seventy shouts directions in Dutch.

Suddenly I turn and there is one of Rachel's ten children, Reuben. "Oh, you're here for the candy scramble? Good! It's a lot of fun to watch the pre-scholars," he says. We find Benuel in the ring of children, and Reuben, Ike Riehl, his brother-in-law, and I stand behind him.

The woman's directions in Dutch get more urgent and the circle of children is squirmy, ready to spring. She and an old, white-haired Amishman using a cane carry a shiny chrome washbasin full of candy into the center of the circle. One little boy of about four bolts for the candy and the crowd roars as he is restrained by his mother. Across the circle another child, this time a girl of about five, does the same thing. Again, laughter. And a third child, a boy of about fourteen with Down's syndrome heads out, and his father hugs him, standing behind the boy with a big smile as the adults behind him say in English, laughing, "Where do you think *you're* going?" There is no embarrassment or reluctance to have this big boy included in the circle of little children. The Amish believe that "special children" are God's angels in disguise. A family receiving such a child is considered blessed.

The count of three is in English. Then: "GO!"

But not one child moves.

The circle of adults behind the circle of children leans in and pushes the children on like a great wave. Girls bend over and gather up handfuls of candy. Rachel's youngest daughter, Susie, leans in and tells the child in front of her to put the candy in her apron and go on gathering more. It is very quiet. If this were any place else, little children would be yelling and climbing all over each other to grab as much candy as possible. But here, the scramble is subdued.

Ike and Reuben squat down, lean in, and tell Benuel, who is in a daze, to gather candy and put it in his hat.

Benuel takes off his little straw hat and there is a gasp. "Benuel, what happened?" a number of people ask in Dutch. Ike Riehl asks in English, chuckling but amazed. His wife, standing nearby, starts laughing too. Benuel looks up at them both as if caught with his pants down. (Several days before, while Levi and Katie were in the barn milking, Rebecca fetched a large pair of scissors from a drawer in the kitchen and gave Benuel a haircut.)

"Benuel looks like he could be *your* son," Ike Riehl says to me, laughing. Reuben starts laughing too. This is not quite an insult. Benuel *and* Rebecca will be chided for weeks—until Benny's hair grows completely back.

After he has gathered up candy, Benuel is still overwhelmed by the whole thing. "I got candy. I got candy," he says over and over again. The Amish children around him stare at the English friend of an English-looking Amish boy.

Elam comes to the candy scramble. Rachel hands him a big bag of balloons and in Dutch tells him to give one to each of their forty-three grandchildren. Elam walks to the crowd. By now the scramble and the baseball games are over. The men stand in a large huddle of about fifty. Some are smoking, others have taken off their hats and are holding them with both hands in front of them. Directly opposite sits a huge circle of women in lawn chairs. Children are wandering through both groups. Adolescents sit in the shade of a huge tree.

There is a kind of settling in. People are quieter. I watch an Englishman of about thirty-six in black jeans and a white shirt talking to a man who could be his double but for his Amish hat, beard, and suspendered pants. I think of stories about twins or doubles and people trading places as these two might. Maybe they are brothers.

While Elam passes out colored balloons to his grandchildren, I go to the Horizon and write letters with the windows rolled up and the radio playing. I am so obviously out of place, feeling both awkward and mesmerized, that it's hard not to gape. WITF, the public radio station in Harrisburg, is playing a Chopin prelude. The music is gentle and full of grace, like the reunion.

Elam walks to the car. He is not one for crowds. "That's enough," he declares. "Let's perk." We drive to Lancaster to fill a prescription for Elam's heart medicine.

A lone yellow balloon hangs over the Smucker farm against a milky blue, late afternoon sky. Elam looks up. "Well, I'll be," he says. "It must be from one of the grandchildren."

PART THIRTEEN

Between us and you there is a great gulf

fixed. . . .   —Luke 16:26

◆

The lamp is lit.

I am sitting in a rocker by the bedroom window facing Belmont Road. Across the road people are gathered in Aaron Lapp's farmhouse.

They are singing to God.

Levi and Katie are there. Levi's deep baritone voice blows with the wind across the fields and into the bedroom window. It flutters the green shades. In the rumble and howl of a wild June night people are singing to God—calm in a storm.

The singing sounds like Gregorian Chant, sung on 'ah.' It wafts up to a high note, then glides down, like a dove loose in the rafters of a cathedral. It contains the essence of Amish faith. A deep sense of the Lord at hand. Reverent, austere, beautiful, sincere, human, deep.

"Certain thoughts are prayers," Victor Hugo wrote. "There are moments when, whatever be the attitude of the body, the soul is on its knees."

It is a wild, lonely night. Elam and Rachel are snoring in the next room. I sit in the rocker—my soul, like those in Aaron Lapp's farmhouse, on its knees.

◆

I have now been with the Stoltzfuses for seventy-two days. At five this morning we rise. I put on my socks and boots on the way to the barn to help Katie and Levi with morning milking.

Sometime last week Levi asked if I wanted to go to church with his family. When I told Rachel she beamed, saying, "You mean he asked you? Good! Now you can go! See, it won't do for Elam as a minister to bring you. But you can go with the younger people." The last thing Elam needs is to walk into service with an Englishman from Harvard trailing behind him.

After chaining each cow to its proper stall and feeding the calves with a bottle and putting hay in the outside bins and shooing reluctant cows into their respective pastures once they've been milked, and after brushing crotchety Pat for Rachel and Elam's carriage, I wash my hair with cold water under a spigot and join Rachel and Elam for breakfast—as every day, two fried eggs in warm milk and margarine, toast, cereal with a piece of chocolate cake plopped in the middle of the bowl, and, for me, instant coffee.

I sit on the couch in Katie's sitting room in a blue blazer and khaki pants and white shirt and blue Rooster tie, with (by now) a thick beard, Amish style, while Katie brushes Benuel's hair. Rebecca is in a simple aqua dress with a white sheer apron and bonnet; Katie is in a black dress; Levi, barefoot, comes out in his white shirt and black pants, fastening his suspenders.

Elam and Rachel head up the Belmont Road with the team at about 7:15 A.M. At the house of the family whose turn it is to host church there are about ten carriages parked on the lawn at the side of the house. The men and boys line the walls of the open garage, standing in the order of their arrival. When we walk in, the talk stops. We go around shaking everyone's hand. The oldest man present, the district bishop, says, "You've brought a stranger, Levi." I say good morning reservedly to everyone. Because we are the last to arrive we stand on the outside right of the garage. Women bustle in and out of the side kitchen door. Some carry Tupperware containers. The horses are all hitched near a haywagon that has hay spread for them on it.

We go into the basement of a 1950s-style suburban two-story house that has been "converted"—electrical wiring removed, a brown linoleum floor laid, the walls painted light blue, and green shades hung from the windows. There are two sets of benches and chairs set up, facing the center of the room, and a center aisle dividing the room in half. Men and women sit separately, facing each other. The three ministers for the service sit in front, in chairs with backs. I can see Rachel in the front row of women, who, like the men, are seated from front to back according to age and marital status. Because Levi is with an outsider he is sitting with me at the back of the room. No one sits in the vacant place to my left. Copies of the *Ausbund*, the Amish hymnal, are on all the benches.

A man announces a song from the *Ausbund*. He sings the first word of each line and then the whole congregation joins in. We sing about five verses from two different songs, and this lasts about twenty minutes. The singing is slow, each syllable extended and dolorous. The songs describe the martyrdom of the earliest Anabaptists in Europe.

When the songs have concluded there is a long pause. Two babies are crying, a little boy in the men's section on one side of the basement, a little girl in the women's section. A man with a squared-off beard pours a glass of water which is passed to the little boy, who stops crying.

The oldest man present is a bishop, in a black coat like Elam's with a longer, pointier white beard and long fingers. He latches his left thumb to his pants. In a thin but stern voice he addresses the congregation in Dutch. On occasion he stops, pausing, then resumes with an "And ahh . . ." getting back into his rhythm. The room is very hot. A man in the back of the room is snoring. The children are antsy.

Elam stands and recites entirely from memory what I will later learn is the parable of Lazarus and Dives. At times his recitation and sermon become so passionate that he sings it like a cantor might, on a high, continuous note, barely stopping for breath.

"There was a certain rich man," the parable begins, "which was clothed in purple and fine linen, and fared sumptuously every day. And there was a certain beggar named Lazarus, which was laid at his gate full of sores. And desiring to be fed with the crumbs which fell from the rich man's table: moreover the dogs came and licked his sores.

"And it came to pass that the beggar died, and was carried by the angels into Abraham's bosom: the rich man also died and was buried.

"And in hell he lift up his eyes, being in torments, and seeth Abraham afar off, and Lazarus in his bosom.

"And he cried and said, Father Abraham, have mercy on me, and send Lazarus, that he may dip the tip of his finger in water, and cool my tongue: for I am tormented in this flame. But Abraham said, Son, remember that thou in thy lifetime receivedst thy good things, and likewise Lazarus evil things: but now, is comforted and thou art tormented. And beside all this, between us and you there is a great gulf fixed: so that they which would pass from hence to you cannot; neither can they pass to us, that would come from hence.

"Then he said, I pray thee therefore, father, that thou wouldest send him to my father's house: for I have five brethren: that he may testify unto them, lest they also come into this place of torment.

"Abraham said unto him. They have Moses and the prophets; let them hear them. And he said, Nay, father Abraham: but if one went unto them from the dead they will repent. And he said unto him if they hear not Moses and the prophets, neither will they be persuaded, though one rose from the dead."

Elam's message is simple and powerful: take nothing for granted concerning your salvation. Just because you are the member of a congregation is no guarantee of membership in the Kingdom. There is no automatic entrance to heaven. Our deeds can betray us. It is a sermon he will give often, albeit in a slightly altered version, worried as Elam is that his people "have gone soft."

Then the deacon reads in a sad voice from Luke 17, the story of the ten lepers. To underscore Elam's point that one should not take one's membership within a faith community as automatic salvation, the deacon emphasizes the fact that the nine who ran off after being cleansed by Jesus were Jews and that the one who returned in thanks was an "auslander"—a Samaritan, an "outsider."

Twice during the service the people turn around and rest their folded hands on the benches as they kneel in silence, facing away from the center of the room. The room is now still. Not even the sound of children. Benuel has long gone to sleep on the cool floor under a bench.

We sing about four verses of another song which again lasts about twenty minutes. Then the youngest boys file out, bench by bench. They stop as they fetch their brimmed, black-felt hats from a table piled with hats at the door. In less than five minutes the older men have adeptly stacked the benches, creating one long table. Levi, another man, and I gather up hymnals and put them in two brown chestlike wooden boxes. The entire service has lasted almost three hours.

The men sit down for a light meal served by the women. Elam and the bishop are at the head of the table. To Elam's right is the sad-voiced deacon. Benuel wedges himself between the deacon and Elam, much to Elam's delight. There are about thirty men and boys at this first sitting. Levi and I stand at the back of the room to wait our turn.

Silence. But three men at the back of the room are still talking. The bishop regards them and waits until they see that he is looking at them.

Now, silence. All present bow their heads, hands folded in laps. A wall clock ticking. A baby breathing heavily through caked little nostrils. After a minute the bishop and Elam let out a long sigh and everyone looks up. The men are poured coffee and tea by five women and girls who bustle through serving. The men will eat in two shifts. When they are finished, then the women will eat.

Several of the older men present, those not seated, ask me where I'm from and do I understand Dutch and what is the weather like this time of year in Boston, and a younger man who works on a construction crew says, "Oh Boston, home of the Red Sox, huh?"

Standing waiting to eat I thank Levi, saying, "I know this must put you in a funny place with your own people," and Levi says "Well, it sort of does, but for me the benefits are worth it." And once again as I seem to be doing constantly this summer, I tell him I am very grateful.

At the table we eat chunky, sweet soft yellow bread, peanut butter with molasses swirled into it, jelly, "smearcase" (homemade cheese spread), lunchmeat, and cold, cold well water. While I am gulping down my third glass of water at the table, Elam walks by holding his hat. Time to perk. I will be riding home with Elam and Rachel

because Levi and Katie are going to visit relatives of Katie's after the meal.

I jump up, help Elam hitch Pat to the carriage and we pull around for Rachel standing near the kitchen door. Rachel and I roll open the back window of the market wagon (which is actually a canvas flap) so I can see out as Rachel says goodbye to a number of people. A few men are also hitching up their teams, some are already walking home—a man pulls his two little girls down the road in a red wooden wagon.

Elam drives us down the Belmont Road, turning up the field lane to enter the Stoltzfus farm from the rear. He is spent. He stood before the congregation this morning for over an hour reciting and interpreting the parable from Luke 16.

Elam knows the sanctity of his ministry. He tells me that after an Amishman's name is drawn (by lots) and he is thus made a minister for a church district, people offer the chosen man and his wife deep condolences. It is not a time for rejoicing. "Being a minister is harder than farming," Elam tells me. "You farm by day. But you're always a minister. Preaching really wears a man out," he says in a worn voice holding Pat's reins. "You have to make yourself empty so God can fill you up. That takes a lot out of you. People have no *i*-dea what it is to give a sermon. I don't say that to be boastful. But it's the truth just the same."

At Sunday dinner that afternoon, Elam and Rachel's side of the house buzzes with the clinking and chewing of over thirty children and grandchildren present at the table. Elam recalls riding the Number 13 bus into Lancaster to read the German newspapers in the Franklin and Marshall College library earlier in the week. He had wandered out of the library and into the student union, quietly eating the lunch Rachel had packed for him in the corner of its large dining room.

"Then a student, a real nice girl, asked could she sit with me and I said, 'Why sure!'" Elam begins. "She asked me some questions about being Amish—the usual things outsiders want to know—and I asked her what did she study."

Elam pauses. I watch his mind search for a word and a concept completely unfamiliar to him.

"She said she studied—what was that word? Oh yeah! She said she studied 'philosophy.' I asked her what that is. She said they tried to figure out the meaning of life."

Elam's eldest daughter, Rachel, forty-four, the mother of ten children, turns to me while cutting meat on the child's plate to her left and says, "Why? Don't they read the Bible in college?"

"Not usually," I reply, looking into my food. Then there is silence. I look up. Everyone is looking at me. I feel I am the official spokesperson for the outside world. Deep in my heart I am ashamed of the culture I am being asked to interpret.

The gulf between our worlds sometimes seems so vast—and so fixed.

PART FOURTEEN

Then God said, "Let the earth bring forth all kinds
of living things." —Genesis 1:24

◆

One afternoon Levi and I walk into the barn and notice a tiny pink
hoof protruding from the rear of an enormously oversized cow. Instantly, Levi grabs a pair of long plastic gloves. As he yanks, the
white face of a calf slowly emerges between its own two porcelain-
white legs: bloody, making a slow sticky noise. Sweat pours down
Levi's temples, and the cow birthing the calf is bawling for all she
is worth. The other cows in the barn shift uneasily, sensing what is
occurring in their midst.

While all this is happening Levi turns to me and says, panting,
"Creation is a messy business!"

The calf slides from its mother and suddenly plops onto the barn
floor in a black and white heap. Levi bends down, grabs a piece of
straw and tickles the inside of the calf's nose until it sneezes, and
thus, breathes.

Suddenly it is alive.

Levi lifts the calf's leg. "A little bull calf," he says like a proud
father.

Then, hunched over the shiny new life, Levi looks up and asks,
"Isn't it a mystery?"

◆

Lying in bed the same evening the calf has been born, I am both-
ered. I keep thinking about the word "mystery" Levi used, and about

the Amish. It is very late; both Elam and Rachel are fast asleep. I throw on my clothes and walk barefoot into the meadow to see the new bull calf standing in the moonlight. It is well after two A.M. The bull stands clean and new with his mother at the far end of the meadow, as far away from the barn as they could be. There is no traffic on the roads. The trucks have all long gone. It is so still I can hear the steady, sandpaper rhythm of the cow's tongue on the little bull's hide.

I think of the fact that the word "witness" has to do with evidence or signs or indications of something. As do this cow and calf. And Levi. I think of Levi in the barn earlier today, and of words that Dorothy Day once quoted from the Archbishop of Paris: "To be a witness does not consist in engaging in propaganda or even in stirring people up, but in being a living mystery; it means to live in such a way that one's life would not make sense if God did not exist." *

I stand barefooted thinking of Elam. Earlier in the week, he and I trooped across the Franklin and Marshall College campus to the library to look for some maps of the county. In lieu of classes, campus had been taken over for the summer. Everywhere there were boys in soccer gear and coaches in black shorts and white and black striped shirts blowing whistles and clapping their hands and yelling, "Atta boy! Good work! Good WORK!"

Elam and I had just driven in from the farm. I had been up since five working in the sweltering barn, where I am regularly stung in the eyes by sweat rolling off my head. My white shirts are permanently stained yellow. I have gained ten pounds and back muscles. I sleep so soundly in the Stoltzfus house I sometimes awaken myself with my own snoring. So for all that, hearing the word "work" in the context of a soccer camp seemed like complete insanity.

Elam turned to me and asked, "What is this?"

"It's a soccer camp," I said. I felt my soul tense.

"What is 'soccer'?" Elam asked blank-faced.

"It's a sport. Like baseball." (I knew some Amish played baseball at family outings.) "These boys are here to learn how to play it better," I replied quickly.

*Coles, Robert, *Dorothy Day: A Radical Devotion*, Reading, Mass.: Addison-Wesley, 1987, page 160.

"But why? It's a *game*," Elam said, puzzled.

"These boys have paid money to come here to learn how to play a sport better," I repeated tersely.

"But why would they go to school to learn a sport?" he persisted.

"Because the outside world doesn't have or *value* productive, meaningful work for its young men, so it teaches them that it's important to know how to play a sport well. This keeps them occupied until they go to college and THEN THEY PAY A LOT OF MONEY TO COME HERE AND ASK WHAT IS THE MEANING OF LIFE!!!"

I practically turned on him—and my own world. I shocked Elam with my vehemence. I shocked myself as well. I wondered what was happening to my view of the world.

Now, standing in Levi's meadow in the middle of the night, suddenly I understand what has happened. At this hour, in this stillness, among these people, life makes perfect sense. The outside world does not. I have become a witness.

I return to the upstairs bedroom as the blue mantel clock in Elam and Rachel's room chimes three, and fall asleep to a cow lowing in the moonlight.

PART FIFTEEN

Go and assemble the elders . . . and tell them . . . I am
concerned about you and about the way you
are being treated. —Exodus 3:16

◆

What the Amish *really* think (and who is in a position to know what
they really think) is a political football hurled from one end of Lancaster County's political spectrum to the other. At times it seems
there are more spokespeople for the Amish than there are Amish.
It is difficult to glean a representative opinion from the Amish on
certain issues because the Amish reserve their deepest feelings for
their own people or in some cases for the selected few outsiders they
trust; nonetheless, many outsiders are eager to align Amish sentiments with their own political and moral agendas. They claim to
know those sentiments and then use them for their own purposes.

Publicly, the Amish choose vague language and sometimes appear wishy-washy. This is purposeful. They are keenly aware of
their significance in the county. Remembering their own history in
Europe, and the history of the Mennonites in Russia—favored by
the government at first but eventually banished for their economic
success as farmers—the Amish are ever mindful that if they "put
themselves over others" dire consequences could follow. They are
also acutely sensitive to being manipulated by outsiders.

When, for example, PENNDoT consultant Watt Bowie came to
Abraham Blank's house seeking Blank's assistance in orchestrating
a quiet meeting between the Amish and PENNDoT, Blank wanted to

know if there would also be unpublicized meetings between PENN-DoT and Catholics, between PENNDoT and Lutherans, and between PENNDoT and Jews. "Why are *we* being singled out?" Blank asked.

Blank knew the Amish were being maneuvered into a position where they would be fed a series of leading questions (without reporters or others to observe), which would be answered by the Amish vaguely, if at all. Then the answers could be used as "findings" to back a new highway. The meetings were never held.

It became impossible for me to read the Lancaster newspapers without getting sick to my stomach, or to hear my Amish friends talk about leaving without feeling ashamed of the outside world, or to ride the train from Philadelphia to Lancaster without noticing yet more tract housing on the landscape, or to hear yet more stories of Amish people being fined or threatened or hit in their buggies or being hectored by tourists without wanting to bang my fists against the sky.

I had talked to immobilized county bureaucrats, condescending businessmen, and oblivious residents. I was shocked at the fact that oftentimes the people who knew the Amish least were the same people who prided themselves on being native to Lancaster County. But what could be done?

In late August 1989, John Hostetler and I had breakfast at the Bird-in-Hand Restaurant along Route 340. We speculated about what we would need to do to bring Harrisburg and the Plain People together. Then we split the legwork. John inquired among the Amish to see if anyone was interested in the idea; I was responsible for contacting Harrisburg to see what might happen.

Would Governor Robert P. Casey come to supper?

I spoke with Paul Alpaugh, the Governor's deputy administrative assistant, a thirty-three-year-old pragmatist and Villanova University graduate in charge of scheduling trips and appointments. Alpaugh asked who I was and why I was interested in proposing such a dinner.

I assured Alpaugh I wasn't setting up a political ambush. There would be no land-preservation people on hand, there would be no local politicians, no Democrats or Republicans seeking public office; it would just be the Governor, his family, John and Beulah Hostetler, a group of Amish people, and me. Period. I said I thought it would be good if the Governor could hear what was on the minds of some of the oldest residents of the Commonwealth. I told him I had Amish friends in Lancaster County and that I lay awake almost every evening praying that my friends would not have to move from the place they know as their homeland.

With this assurance, the voice on the other end of the line suddenly softened. "I think it's a great idea; I think Governor Casey would be very interested in coming to supper," Alpaugh said. He surveyed Governor Casey's calendar and concluded the supper would have to be in November. Then Alpaugh said, "I'd like to come too."

Paul Alpaugh's challenge to me—why was I so involved?—was offputting but very important. John Hostetler and I had asked the question of ourselves often: spiritual pride is an ongoing temptation in this work.

Were we different from others "concerned" about the Amish? Or were we simply more arrogant?

John Hostetler *is* different. He comes from an Amish background and has spent his whole life writing about the Amish and working on their behalf. He is the gatekeeper between the outside world and the Amish, their long-trusted mediator and friend.

I had worked often with John for over a year. I hadn't come to Lancaster County intending to be some sort of public advocate or activist. I simply came to write my thesis and graduate from the Harvard Graduate School of Education. My "concern" had come by itself—while standing on a haywagon and talking with Levi Stoltzfus or shoveling manure in his barn.

Did we claim to know what the Amish really think?

John Hostetler *does* know. He has been consulted scores of times on behalf of the Amish—once even by the Supreme Court in a case permanently guaranteeing the Amish the right to school their children in their own parochial schools. I felt that under John's tutelage I was beginning to understand how the Amish think.

Were the Amish setting themselves above others—or were we setting them above others—by proposing such a dinner? No. *We* were the ones arranging it, they had not asked us to do it. We were attempting to act as mediators between the world of Harrisburg and the world of the Plain People. And finally, the Amish would be on their own land, with the doors shut, free to say as much or as little as they cared to. There was no agenda except dialogue, Amish-style—close-up and personal—and the breaking of bread.

So we proceeded nervously ahead.

I called John and said, "The Governor's up for it, how about the Amish?" Several days later John visited three Amishmen: Elam Stoltzfus, Abraham Blank, and Benuel Kauffman from Bird-in-Hand, whose farm sits along Route 340 across from a restaurant and miniature golf course—a man who thus has had many experiences with, as he calls them, "our 'guests' to Lancaster County." The Kauffman family agreed to host the supper but was doubtful about having it in November: all Amish weddings in Lancaster County are held on Tuesdays and Thursdays throughout that month.

The dinner would be jointly hosted by the three men and their families. The Governor and his wife, their children, and two of their grandchildren would be guests. And there would be absolutely no publicity. This was requisite for the Amish. The Governor's staff promised no press would be on hand.

On September 20, 1989, the three Amishmen signed this letter, and John Hostetler sent it to the Governor:

As members of the Old Order Amish community we extend to you an invitation to visit us for an afternooon and evening. We would be pleased to have you visit our farms, the country roads, and perhaps a school, and have you come for a meal at our homes.

We would be pleased to discuss with you informally our common concerns in respect to the future of our agricultural way of life in Lancaster County.

We extend to you our best wishes.

On October 23rd, Alpaugh replied:

The Governor has asked me to respond on his behalf to your recent letter inviting him to visit with you.

He has agreed to do so during the late afternoon and early evening of Monday, November 20, 1989. As the date approaches, I will confirm additional details through Randy Testa and Professor Hostetler. . . .

The Governor appreciates your kind invitation and looks forward to learning about the concerns of the Old Order Amish community in Lancaster County.

Between those two letters, Harrisburg lawyer William Ball wrote the Governor a letter of his own, in an attempt to unburden his desk of a mounting caseload involving alleged Amish breaches of environmental code. Ball, whose law office is also the headquarters of the National Committee for Amish Religious Freedom, has long been active on behalf of the Amish. He wrote:

Since September 20th, a series of problems have come to a head which indicate the desirability of a meeting in the relatively near future—a meeting which a small group of Amish bishops and leaders would be most willing to attend at your office at a time convenient to you. Such a meeting is now rather urgently needed because of the growing number of environmental problems which the Amish are encountering, especially in the "Amish country" of Lancaster County. Let me explain:

Our Amish are very law-abiding people, as you know. They are famous for always "working with nature," not against nature. They respect the environment and desire to comply with all reasonable laws protecting the environment. Of recent years, however, they have faced numerous enforcement actions, by local Department of Environmental Regulation officials, with which they have encountered very real difficulties so far as compliance is concerned.

Noting that the Amish have been quite successful, on the whole, in managing their farms in ways protective of the environment, it has seemed to us that the application of *some* DER regulations to the Amish may not be necessary where they entail extreme expense to them or technological changes which the Amish cannot accept. Moreover, given the simple Amish life style, it would seem appropriate for DER to entertain alternative environ. mental proposals set forth by the Amish. I see a major difference between industrial pollution and some of the kinds of variations from DER requirements for which traditional Amish farm and household management call.

My plea, hence, is that you would be willing to meet with a small group of spokesmen for the Amish community in order to discuss briefly the possibility of less stringent approaches by DER in relation to the Amish farmlands. We would naturally hope that the Secretary of DER be present.

We feel that your personal chairing of such a meeting would be essential for two reasons: (a) You are governor of the state which has the oldest concentration of Amish citizens in the United States. Our Pennsylvania Amish are, in a sense, a national heritage, and it is important that the Commonwealth's chief executive be knowledgeable respecting their life and needs. (b) I feel that your personally taking an interest in their present concerns will help DER better to see that this matter is not a routine environmental matter but one that is special and deserves extraordinary consideration.

Ball's letter was responsible for significantly altering the tenor of the upcoming dinner. Several days after the Governor received it, Paul Alpaugh contacted John Hostetler with a request from the Governor: might the Amish bishops also be on hand for the supper in order that Casey might hear for himself what Ball had detailed in his letter?

Hostetler went back to the three hosts. Benuel Kauffman was surprised by the change in number. "This thing has gotten kind of out of hand now," he said, scratching his head. "I stuck my foot in my mouth by saying I'd do this. But then I say to myself, 'Imagine, Benny! The Governor of Pennsylvania would pay attention to the likes of us.' And it makes me have hope."

A list of Amish bishops who might be willing to attend was drawn up. Then John Hostetler and Elam Stoltzfus criss-crossed the Amish portion of Lancaster County in John's Honda Civic— through Morgantown, New Providence, Mascot, Paradise, Witmer, Christiana, Georgetown, and Bird-in-Hand, paying calls on all of the bishops whose names were on the list. And even though the dinner would be held in the middle of "wedding season" all ten bishops agreed to come.

Benuel's wife, Sarah, worried where she would get so many extra chairs.

There were other concerns as well.

During one telephone conversation Alpaugh mentioned that it was routine for the Governor's staff to carry weapons whenever Casey traveled by motorcade. But for this dinner it was agreed that all guns would be kept in the trunks of cars and that the Governor's driver and bodyguards would be unarmed and would remain in the kitchen during supper. Several days before the supper, Alpaugh and Hostetler walked the grounds of Benuel Kauffman's farm assessing it for security.

The Governor's Office called John Hostetler to find out what might be appropriate gifts for the hosting families.

Levi Stoltzfus debated whether or not he would attend. Because Katie is rather shy, she decided to stay home with the children.

I wrote Alpaugh a list of Amish table customs so the Caseys would know what to do and what was going on. (For example, after the Amish are finished eating their dinner they scrape their plates clean with their spoons and forks. The din and intensity with which this is accomplished can seem overwhelming.)

Benuel and Sarah Kauffman handed me a list of errands to do by car on the day of the dinner, such as, "pick up shoo-fly pies." Supper would commence at five. Sarah Kauffman got metal-and-wooden folding chairs from the Gordonville Fire Hall. All the table leaves in the house were put into her kitchen table so it could be set for thirty-eight. Early on the morning of November 20th the special "wedding soup" the Amish make from celery was bubbling in a big pot on Sarah Kauffman's stove. Benuel frantically ran around his farm tidying everything, as did his sons. I picked up the six shoo-fly pies an Amish neighbor had made.

At two-thirty in the afternoon, a navy-blue, four-door Ford LTD slowly pulled into the parking lot of the tourist attractions across from the Kauffman farm, then came to a halt. A member of the Governor's security staff wearing a navy-blue suit and sunglasses sat inside the car. The Kauffmans waved to him from across the road and sent me over to ask if he'd had his dinner yet or would he like me to bring some along.

◆

The Governor was due to arrive at the Kauffman farm at five but decided to wait until his entire family was gathered in Harrisburg. After they all had arrived, they headed out together in a motorcade of three navy-blue Ford LTDs, forty minutes late.

The Amish arrived early—as they always will—at four thirty. The bishops crowded into the sitting room, where they sat along with Elam and Abraham Blank, tense, hardly speaking. The women worked in the kitchen chatting and laughing, mashing potatoes or stirring the contents of large, shiny metal pots.

At 5:40 P.M. the Governor's motorcade pulled into the Kauffman farm, slowly crunching on the gravel driveway. They parked alongside a dozen Amish buggies. Governor Casey stepped out. He is a tall, white-haired, good-looking man, intense in a way that lets you know he has been involved with the vicissitudes of politics for a long, long time. The Governor wore a blue pin-striped suit, and Mrs. Casey wore a blue-and-white dress. They walked in carrying three copies of a book titled *Pennsylvania Historic Places* under their arms.

Benuel and Sarah greeted the Governor at the side door of their farmhouse. Then the Governor's family filed in behind him and they all headed into the sitting room. The Governor went straight over to the bishops, all of whom wore cobalt-blue shirts and black vests, and shook their hands. None of the bishops stood up. Levi and I sat in wooden chairs in a corner of the room. We stood when we shook hands with the Governor.

The Governor's children were all slightly older or younger than Levi and me. They chatted animatedly to the Amish, and when Jack and Casey, two of the Governor's grandchildren (both aged eight) walked in wearing blue blazers and ties, the women fussed over them, the men smiled, the awkwardness began to melt, and supper was off and running.

Benuel asked everyone to be seated at the table. The water glasses said HOOBER FEED MILLS on them and the metal folding chairs had the words GORDONVILLE FIRE CO. stenciled in white paint on their backs. The long table was spread for a feast, beautiful in its utter modesty. There was much movement back and forth from table to kitchen.

Governor and Mrs. Casey sat in the middle of one side of the table, flanked by John and Beulah Hostetler, the Casey sons and daughters, their spouses, and the two grandsons. On the other side of the table sat ten Amish bishops, Elam, Abraham Blank and Benuel Kauffman, then the Governor's son, Bobby, his brother-in-law, Jack Walsh, Levi Kauffman, and me. Sarah Kauffman, her daughters and daughters-in-law, and Rachel Kauffman served in the kitchen.

Then Sarah lit three propane lamps and hung them from hooks above the table. Benuel Kauffman went through the gathering, nervously pushing in everyone's chair. Then he said, "It's our way to have a silent prayer before and after we eat." The room became very still.

Benuel bowed his head and closed his eyes. Everyone joined him.

The bishops breathed heavily. In the long, thick silence I opened my eyes. The Caseys were bowed low over the table in their dress clothes. They looked stripped of authority, awed and gentle. Paul Alpaugh, the Governor's chauffeur, and his two gigantic bodyguards were standing in the middle of Sarah Kauffman's kitchen, their eyes closed, heads bowed, their arms across their chests and surrounded by Amish women. I could hear occasional cars whiz by on Route 340. It was dark outside. The white mantels of the lanterns hissed and glowed while the lid of a pot simmering on the stove clattered as bubbles spilled over the top.

Benuel's office chair squeaked and then he sighed a long deep sigh. People opened their eyes slowly, adjusting to the intense light of the three lamps, as if awakening from a dream.

The members of the Casey family introduced themselves and then Abraham Blank (after John Hostetler whispered a reminder in his ear) asked the bishops to "tell your name and how many children you have." This took some time. The Caseys remarked at the number of Amish represented by these ten bishops. It was well over a hundred. Then Jack McGrath, the Governor's grandson, recited a short German prayer by heart. Everyone clapped and the Amish fussed over him for the rest of the night.

Rachel, Sarah Kauffman, and her daughters and daughters-in-law began to serve the meal. Rachel walked saucily among the members of the Casey family, saying things to the men like: "You look like you could eat this whole plate!" and "This isn't a night to be shy!" or "Take some more chicken! There's plenty more where that came from!" her eyes flashing the entire time. When she came my way, I whispered in her ear something I'd heard Katie say to Benuel and Rebecca, "You're really something, you know that?" Elam was quiet and rather awed, looking much like his grandson Benuel did at the candy scramble the summer before.

"This," Sarah Kauffman said for the Caseys' benefit, "is a wedding meal since November is wedding month for us."

Chicken, gravy, stuffing, celery soup, mashed potatoes, cole slaw, plates of celery sticks and carrots, corn, applesauce, warm bread, "spreading" cheese, jelly, butter, pickles, beets, and much more

was passed around the table. The Caseys were delighted. They stuffed themselves with wide eyes as they worried aloud about their diets and inquired as to what was in certain dishes. They asked child-like questions about Amish life and customs while the Amish politely asked them about their families.

When the dishes were cleared by the Amish women, Benuel stood up and invited Abraham to say a few words. The Amish are not good at such ceremony. They don't employ it at their own gather-ings, so this forced formality on behalf of the Governor was awkward and painful, a measure of the earnestness and sincerity the supper was being accorded. Levi was sitting next to me in his best black suit with grease under his fingernails and tiny flecks of straw in the corners of his spectacles in contrast to the Caseys, who all looked scrubbed and neat. We were squashed together on a long bench used for church. With Levi so near at hand, I felt comforted, grateful.

Abraham stood up and gathered his thoughts for a minute. He traced the history of the Amish in Lancaster County from their mas-sacre by Indians in Berks County in the 1700s to today. He said that the Amish have grown from six districts to ninety-two. He stopped and said, "Today we wonder how long we can remain here." At this, the bishops looked at one another gravely. They were silent.

Abraham sat down and Benuel Kauffman stood up. He said that the tourist trade in Lancaster County began in the 1950s when the Brunswick Hotel in Lancaster took a group of tourists through the countryside on a bus ride. He said, "Tourism brings some good things, but also some bad things come along with it." He described "all the things that have come here in its wake."

Listening to Benuel Kauffman describe housing developments being built everywhere, the Governor leaned forward. When Benuel was finished the Governor asked, "Doesn't zoning work for you?"

The ten Amish bishops chuckled. They glanced at each other as if to say, "Poor man! He doesn't understand how law-making in Lancaster County works."

Now the Governor was about to receive a combined lesson in civics and theology. Sensing the Governor's confusion, Benuel Kauffman explained, "It's not our way, Governor, to serve on township commissions." And a bishop at the far end of the table added, "Besides, some township officials are developers themselves."

The Governor optimistically described the Commonwealth's recently mandated $100 million farmland-preservation program. It encourages farmers thinking about selling their farms to developers to strike a compromise with the Commonwealth instead: they sell to the state and receive a compensatory price for the land that falls somewhere between the price the farm would fetch if it remained in farming and what it would fetch on the development market. The Commonwealth then offers the farm for sale to another farmer, at an adjusted current price for land in farming. This keeps the farm in production.

Essentially, the program is a subsidy.

Casey said with some pride that the program had been approved by a 2:1 landslide vote and that he was "very hopeful about its effects on the state's farmland."

This was the gift that Casey had intended to present to the Amish community for the evening. Then Abraham Blank leaned across the table, looked the Governor right in the eye, and said quietly and very directly, "But you see, it's not our way to accept government handouts."

The Governor looked very surprised.

After a long pause he asked, "What *would* be suitable?"

Abraham described the efforts of a realtor from Georgia named Nelson Griffith to show the Amish how to draw up a land covenant among themselves saying they would not sell their farms for development. But Elam Stoltzfus then raised an important point: would such a convenant be legally binding in the courts?

"In Georgia covenants have legislative backing," he said. "Would they here? Mr. Ball said he didn't know if they would."

"That's something we could find out about and help you do something with," the Governor replied.

Abraham then went down the line of bishops, calling on each like a wise schoolmaster. "What about you, _____? What do *you* have to say?"

The first bishop began slowly. "Well," he said, "I came mainly to listen. There's been a lot of good points made here tonight. There's plenty to think about. But to my way of thinking it's too late for a covenant."

The Governor unfolded his hands.

The bishop continued, "It's something that should have been done twenty years ago. But it's too late now. My farm has houses on one side of it, a drive-up bank on the other, and railroad tracks behind it. What would I be doing to my children in passing on a farm like that?"

A second bishop with wide eyes said, "I have neighbors from New York who complain whenever I haul manure."

Abraham talked about two farmers who had been fined by the Fish and Game Commission for manure runoff.

The youngest bishop present, who sat pulling at his beard during all the after-dinner talk, had the last word. "The way I see it," he began, "we're in the Lord's hands. And if we lead a godly life, God will provide." With these sentiments, a large book seemed to shut with a thud.

Benuel Kauffman looked around at his people, saying, "Maybe we could sing?" He consulted with his wife in Dutch, then announced, "Blest Be The Tie That Binds." The Amish gathered together and stood at the front of the dining room, some with their eyes closed. Benuel invited the Governor and his family to join in. None of the Caseys knew the words so they sat quietly, listening. The Amish sang the slow hymn with placid faces:

Blest Be The Tie That Binds

Blest be the tie that binds
Our hearts in Christian love;
The fellowship of kindred minds
Is like to that above.

Before our Father's throne,
We pour our ardent pray'rs;
Our fears, our hopes, our aims are one,
Our comforts and our cares.

We share our mutual woes,
Our mutual burdens bear;
And often for each other flows
The sympathizing tear.

110

When we asunder part,
It gives us inward pain;
But we shall still be joined in heart,
And hope to meet again.

Light from the three lanterns sputtered. Outside, a November wind stirred. Dried, white-gray cornstalks rattled in brown fields under a starless, navy-blue sky. Mrs. Casey sat very still. There were tears in her eyes. Equally as moved, the Governor leaned forward toward Abraham and asked quietly, "Where do we go from here?"

At the farmhouse door, Governor Casey worried that the bishops might get caught in high winds on the way home. "Will you people be all right?" he asked.

"Surely. Course, if the wind gets too bad, we can always stop at someone's farm and have a rest," a bishop with thick eyebrows said as he stood in the doorway, trying to speak above the rising wind. "Don't you worry about us, Governor." (Casey called John Hostetler the next morning, wondering whether everyone had made it safely home. They had.)

Governor Casey gave Benuel Kauffman, Elam, and Abraham Blank the books he and his wife had brought and talked to Abraham and Elam about setting up a follow-up meeting in Harrisburg. Benuel passed out topcoats to the Caseys, and the Casey women thanked Sarah Kauffman and all the other Amish women with handshakes. Sarah handed the Caseys a paper plateful of leftover chicken and stuffing saying, "This should keep till you get home." Rachel teased Paul Alpaugh, the chauffeur, and the bodyguards about what kind of easy jobs they had that paid them for standing around eating in a kitchen all night. Levi Stoltzfus invited the Governor's sons to stop by during the spring field work, and John Hostetler talked to Abraham Blank softly in Dutch as Beulah helped the other women put dishes away. I stood whispering in a corner to Elam, both of us watching as coats were put on, the Amish bishops fastening their capes and donning their wide-brimmed felt hats, many car doors slammed, teams were hitched, engines started up, horses impatiently shook their reins, people waved goodbye to each other in lamplight across worlds temporarily converged in a farmhouse with a long wooden table and fire-hall chairs, headlights turned out of the

111

driveway in wide arcs straight into the blackness of Route 340 as the Caseys sped west toward Harrisburg in a sleek motorcade, while a long line of Amish bishops in buggies headed home to their farms in the east.

All who had convened were now scattered in the November wind, holding the night in their hands like a sacrament.

PART SIXTEEN

Say "Yes" when you mean "Yes" and "No" when you

mean "No." Anything beyond that is from

the evil one. —Matthew 5:37

◆

The D.M. Stoltzfus Quarry Company of Leola announced intentions
to annex a farm to its quarry sites along Snake Hill Road. Despite
local opposition from farmers living near his quarry, Mike Stoltzfus took his plans to the Upper Leacock Township Board of Supervisors. Pending the outcome, Stoltzfus hung a gigantic American flag
from a flagpole on the site, to dramatize his belief that individuals'
constitutionally guaranteed property rights were being undermined
by land preservationists—something he saw as fundamentally un-
American. What follows is testimony from the hearings considering
an expanded quarry.

The "witness" is a hydrologist testifying on behalf of the annexa-
tion. Questioning the hydrologist from the audience is Reuben Lapp,
an Amish dairy farmer.

LAPP   My name is Reuben Lapp. I live right beside the proposed
quarry. You mentioned state requirements, three hundred feet
away from a proposed dwelling.

WITNESS   That is correct.

LAPP   Do you know how they came to that amount of feet?

WITNESS   I do not know what—*why* the state chose three hundred
feet—is that your question?

LAPP   Yes.

WITNESS   I do not know.

LAPP   Would you feel comfortable with that if *you* lived there—beside the quarry—with three hundred feet? Would you desire that amount, or would you desire, say, a thousand feet? You would live beside the quarry, have a house right beside it.

WITNESS   Well, I would think that the further you lived from an industrial operation, that might be more comfortable than living next to it. I don't doubt that.

LAPP   I'm not sure if I understood everything correctly. The question was, would you desire three hundred feet or a thousand feet?

WITNESS   Would I desire—well, you're asking me—

LAPP   —Three hundred feet setback or a thousand feet setback?

WITNESS   If what I would desire for a regulation?

LAPP   If you lived beside it, yes.

WITNESS   Well, I can't have it both ways. I would desire a three-hundred-feet setback, not a thousand. A thousand-foot setback would make the price of stone be prohibitive.

LAPP   The question was, if you lived beside the quarry, like we do, would you desire a three-hundred-foot setback or a thousand?

WITNESS   I guess until I lived there I can't answer it. But the answer I have given you stands. I understand living next to an industrial site is not as comfortable as living farther away. And I would propose to live farther from an industrial site than near it.

LAPP   So would I. And when we moved there it was an agricultural site, which is not your fault, as far as that's concerned. (Pause) So you won't give me a yes or no answer, then, on that?

WITNESS   My answer as I gave it stands.

LAPP   But not yes or no.

WITNESS   That is correct.

PART SEVENTEEN

Woe to those who enact unjust statutes and who write

oppressive decrees, Depriving the needy of

judgement and robbing my people's poor

of their rights. . . .

—Isaiah 10:1–2

◆

Of the ongoing disputes that precipitated the meeting with Governor Casey, perhaps the ugliest and most complex was the case of Amishman David A. Fisher.

In order to understand how a dispute over a toilet could make its way to the highest offices of the Commonwealth, you have to understand a few key points.

First, the mindset of David Fisher, an Amishman deep in his faith, who also trains and sells horses for a living. This involves judgments about what you can get away with, sometimes convincing another man that a tired mare is actually a spirited trotter. Not always, but often. You have to be able to hold religious nonresistance in a thousand daily manifestations alongside an ability to embellish the truth in order to make a sale.

Second, you have to understand how different the people of southern Lancaster County are from their more northerly neighbors. Many younger Amish families moved south in the late 1970s, willing to farm the less productive hills along the Susquehanna River in order to escape the worldliness of northern farms surrounded by tourism. In some ways, these are, as writer Eric Nordell has observed, "the plainest of the Plain People"—fiercely independent, wary, like their

English neighbors, of outside interference—occasionally more than willing to take matters into their own hands.

In southern Lancaster County, the moral landscape is, at this writing, a little rougher, a little rockier.

Last, you have to try and understand Marvin Stoner, a sewage enforcement officer for twenty-four years. You have to try to understand how his work would color his view of the world, what his moral framework would consist of. Then you might begin to understand how he could repeatedly fine an Amishman with a wife and eight children again and again and again, until he literally drove them out of their home.

◆

Goshen, southern Lancaster County. Early August, 1988.

David Fisher's lamplight is reflected in a mud puddle. For the first time in weeks, it is finally raining—a light mist. The sky rumbles, and there are flashes that light up the hills around Fisher's farm in blazes of blue-white.

David is telling Levi about two of his horses. The two Amishmen slide in and out of English, aware of my presence. But when the talk gets heated, they lapse into Dutch.

Two of David's eight children—boys aged seven and six—put their big toes deliberately in the puddle and then out, in and then out, and then David does likewise, hardly aware of himself in a rhythm that matches this first steady rain of the entire summer, as he talks earnestly to Levi.

After several minutes, David, two of his boys, Levi, and I gather in the horse stalls of David's father-in-law's barn. David explains that his horses will soon move to a new barn he will build on sixteen acres of adjoining land that his father-in-law will subdivide off for him. We are sitting along the white wooden fences that keep the horses penned in. Levi waffles on the price of a gelding and finally David says, "Well make me an offer, Levi!"

Then David talks about the horses he bought last Friday night at the New Holland Sales Stables. When he speaks his eyes look up and around, carefully, narrowly, from under his straw hat.

David's pants are a soft blue denim material, sewn Amish-style.

117

I have never seen this. And sometimes he uses phrases like, "It was kinda weird—" and "I told the guy, 'No problem.'" David wants to know if we'd like to come to the frolic for his barn-raising in about a week. I glance over at Levi, who knows how excited I would be to go, especially since I will be heading back to Boston soon. Levi says, "We'll be there."

Driving home, Levi and I stop at a Turkey Hill Mini-Mart near a dip in a road local folks call "the Buck." We get sandwiches and soda pop, and when we come out the rain has lightened over hilly roads that wind and melt into other roads or cornfields. The skies flash reddish orange, and we can hear the wet, hissy sound of wheels on pavement because we are driving with all the windows down. Sometimes we stick our heads out the windows and say, "Feel that!" to each other over and over again because there has been no rain for weeks, and sometimes there is a carriage and the headlights from the Horizon light up the reflective tape across its back. On this cooling rainy night it is just the Horizon, Levi, and me, snaking our way back to Paradise eating ham sandwiches, drinking ginger ale—Levi with a head full of thoughts about horses, me thinking about the fact that I will actually be going to an honest-to-goodness barn-raising and that in this particular moment life couldn't be any fuller.

◆

Thursday, August 11, 1988. David Fisher's barn-raising.

About fifty Amish and a few non-Amish men and boys are scampering all over the skeleton of a gambrel-roof barn, 100 feet long by 35 feet wide. It will have stalls for twenty-two horses. The air is pierced by the screaming of buzz saws and the thick, pulpy smell of wooden planks being cut in half. Everyone has a white canvas belt around his waist bulging with nails. The sound of hammering rifles through the wooded glen in which the barn sits.

When we arrive, men are raising part of the high arched frame. On a signal in Dutch given by a young man with a long blond beard, ten men positioned along the frame start to walk toward the other end of the barn while their hands go higher over their heads and the frame shoots into the sky. I am surprised that three ten-year-old boys hold the long pole with a spike at its tip which in turn steadies the frame as it is nailed into place in a flurry of swift hammering by older men. David holds the other pole and surveys the progress on his barn. As always, he is barefoot.

I don't really know what I'm doing.

David comes along a moment later. He points to an Amishman about my age who is putting nails lightly into the sills with one swing of his hammer. The man walks to the next place and does the same thing, all along the wooden base of the barn where it attaches to a cement-block foundation. David says, "Follow him and pound." My job is to hammer in the nails the rest of the way. It takes me many short hits, just like the ten-year-old boys. Levi, I notice, can drive in a nail with just three wide pounds of his hammer.

By 11 A.M. it is well past 90 degrees. But unlike a regular construction crew, no one here has pulled off his shirt. I am constantly wiping sweat out of my eyes.

At 11:15 somebody yells "KOMM ESSE," which even I know by now means "COME EAT!" Everyone drops what he is doing. Many of us hop onto a wooden haywagon pulled by a neighbor's Percherons and take a ride up from the wooded hollow alongside the little creek. The wagon rumbles down a newly made gravel driveway leading up from the site of the barn, out to Sawmill Road to David's father-in-law's barn. There, about twenty men and boys are washing in silence. All there is to be heard is the steady trickle of water into a pewter-colored trough as men wash their Popeyelike arms in clear, cold water, passing around a mushy bar of white soap, stepping aside, waiting to be handed one of a number of cloth towels from men who have already dried themselves off.

Then we file into David's side of his father-in-law's house. David sits at the head of the table, surrounded by his boys, all of whom are barefoot like their father, then teenage boys, then men. David's wife, Sarah, and four other women, wives of other men here today, are scooping food onto large serving dishes. The whole kitchen smells like turkey and everybody is starving.

David bows his head. The clock strikes the half hour and in the stillness I can hear a wooden tick-tock, tick-tock. Birds outside chirp, a man across the table from me clears his throat. I hear the rhythmic breathing of men and boys who had been hammering away in hot sun, and think of Millet's painting *The Angelus.*

David sighs. Everyone seated at the table dives into the macaroni, applesauce, mashed potatoes, turkey with gravy, carrot sticks, thick, sweet chunky wheat bread, butter and jelly, pickles, fresh peaches, cake, apple crisp, cornstarch pudding, and coffee that fly up and down the table. No one talks; the food is too good. When the meal is through, there isn't a scrap of food left. And everybody's plates are as clean as if they'd been put under the table for the barn cats to lick.

David hitches up the big haywagon again and we ride back to the barn in the glen. When it is time for Levi and me to head back to Paradise for evening milking I shake hands with David and thank him for the meal. "Thanks to you," David says, emphasizing the last word. "You'll have to come back when it's all finished."

"That's a promise," I say.

◆

The next time I heard about David Fisher was in a February 9, 1989, *Lancaster Intelligencer Journal* article sent to me in Boston by John Hostetler. The paper reported that Drumore Township Zoning Officer Kathy Morris and Sewage Enforcement Officer Marvin Stoner would be issuing a cease-and-desist order to stop David Fisher from completing work on his barn. I was surprised to read that Fisher intended to use the top floor of the barn as a house for Sarah and their eight children. I hadn't heard anything about this at the frolic in August.

Soon after the article appeared, John Hostetler drove to Goshen to visit the Fishers. Afterward he wrote to the Department of Environmental Resources:

I visited the Fisher family on learning of their problem. They asked for my "help."

The Fishers have purchased some land from Mrs. Fisher's father and applied for a subdivision some months ago. They applied for permission to construct a barn and received approval. They applied for a sewage permit and it has been held up.

It is customary for Amish people to build a barn and to temporarily occupy a part of the structure until the house is built. The family has rented a portable toilet service for as long as they need it.

Fisher is an organic farmer. The premises are orderly and the place is clean. He is an innovator among his people and enjoys good relationships with his neighbors, and certainly does not wish to overstep the laws.

The reasons for the cease-and-desist order were complex. First, Fisher's father-in-law, Christian Lapp, had not been granted approval for the subdivision of his property but he had gone ahead with it anyway. Second, Fisher had not applied for a sewage permit. Fisher initially had applied for a permit to build a barn, not a house. The barn permit was therefore rescinded by the township.

The secretary of the Township Planning Commission, Denise Young, said she was hopeful that Fisher and the township could work things out. But Stoner sounded an ominous note—one that would amplify over time. He said that even if Fisher obtained an occupancy permit, he would still need a sewage permit before he could move into the house. He also said that because of the slopes on Fisher's property, Fisher would have to install what is called a "sand mound" pyramid septic system—a system built to handle about four hundred gallons of water per day. The Fishers used about thirty-five gallons of water per day. The cost of a sand mound septic system was about five thousand dollars. Instead, Fisher had a Port-a-Potty installed on his property. Fisher thought the price of such a system was ridiculous and refused to have on his place an elaborate contraption that was designed for the needs of a suburban home. Fisher was quoted as saying, "Things were a lot simpler in my father's time. We didn't have all of this." *

But the nagging question was one of intention. Did David Fisher intend from the start to build a single house-barn for his family? Or did he actually plan to build a separate house and barn and, as Hostetler's letter describes the Amish custom, live in the barn only until construction of the house was completed? Or, perhaps, did he initially plan two separate structures but then run out of money and decide to move into the barn permanently? Did Fisher inten-

* Woodcock, James A., "Amishman Faces Crisis in House-barn," *Lancaster Intelligencer Journal*, February 9, 1989.

121

tionally deceive the township, or did he change his mind, oblivious to local ordinance? These unanswered questions would plague the subsequent unfolding of events.

◆

It is important to understand the environmental backdrop against which this story is set. In early 1989, several Amishmen were fined for manure runoff violations. This sent shock waves through the Old Order community; there was great concern that people might be regulated right off their farms. Thus, on January 18, 1989, a meeting arranged by John Hostetler was held in an Amish home. On hand were twenty Amish elders, representatives of the Pennsylvania Dutch Visitors' Bureau and the Lancaster County Planning Commission. After describing the recent fines leveled at Amishmen and proposed restrictive ordinances whose enforcement seemed imminent, the Amish talked openly about leaving Lancaster County.

A week later Hostetler summarized the meeting in a letter to William Ball. With uncharacteristic alarm, Hostetler wrote:

Two Amish farmers have been arrested for breach of environmental codes by the Fish and Game Commission. . . . The first farmer is very fearful that he will be cited each day and will have to pay $100 per day, and that if he does not pay he will eventually lose his farm. He wants his son to take over the farm, but with this "arbitrary and unreasonable" action the son will not want to become a farmer. The farmer feels, as do other Amish persons, that "city" folks who have purchased a lot of ground nearby and who have now worked their way into the position of township supervisors are the ones who are now bringing complaints resulting in their arrests. . . .

What is distressing to the Amish is not tourism directly, but the consequences of tourism—folks from all over the nation who want to live in Lancaster County, and industry that wants to locate in the county aggressively promoted by the Chamber of Commerce.

The consequence of this is illustrated by the family from New Jersey who fell in love with Lancaster County, purchased an acre of land, and built a house. The couple was disturbed at four o'clock in the morning by the bellowing of a cow out their bedroom window. They brought suit against the farmer.

I see a whole flood of regulations coming down on farmers in the county, and some of it is coming from the strict enforcement of environmental regulations. There are manure-management regulations coming down the pike, the number of livestock and poultry a farmer is to have, etc. The Amish know they can improve in some ways, but if the regulations are too imposing they will just give up and move out.

There is talk about licensing horse-drawn vehicles. In western Pennsylvania there is agitation to ban Amish buggies and steel wheels on public roads, and in Minnesota the court has ruled the white reflective tape on the rear of buggies insufficient.

If farming is to survive as a viable enterprise, then there ought to be a recognition of "right to farm" legislation. Farmers cannot conduct their affairs if they are ruled by codes made for the convenience of city people.

Several weeks later a summary essay of the same meeting was published in an Amish newspaper. Written by the Amishman hosting the meeting, it warned: "This report is true, and we would better get awake before it is too late. Such incidents we sometimes read about from foreign countries, but this is the United States, the land of freedom."

"Are we awake?" the Amish author asked his people.

On February 23, 1989, Elizabeth Place, a colleague of William Ball's, wrote an in-house memorandum, titled "Farmland Regulations." Place discussed the adversarial climate that had broken out between some local township officials and Amish farmers, and the necessity for educating the Amish about ordinances and their capacity to comply or seek exception to them:

Environmental statues have not historically been strictly enforced against farmers. However, recent events have combined to focus attention on the environmental impact of farming practices, particularly in Lancaster County. Pennsylvania Governor Robert Casey has very publicly endorsed the interstate Chesapeake Bay Program, the goal of which is to end upstream pollution, particularly in Pennsylvania, which is harming the Chesapeake Bay. Nutrient pollution from manure and fertilizers is a major cause of the problem and, since Lancaster County is home to 25 percent of the livestock in Pennsylvania, it is a focal point for cleanup efforts. Additionally, Lancaster County is the site of intense development pressure. The influx of both residential and industrial development in rural Lancaster County has resulted in conflicting uses of the land. Since enforcement of environmental legislation is mostly complaint oriented, an increasing number of citations can be expected. . . .

Some farmers are under the erroneous assumption that the so-called "right to farm" legislation protects their current farming practices. This legislation, which protects normal operations from nuisance suits, does not exempt practices which "have a direct adverse impact on the public health and safety" or which violate government statutes or regulations and does not prohibit recovery for damages sustained as the result of water pollution. . . . [3 P.S. §951 *et. seq.*]

Regulation of farming practices presents an ongoing problem for the Amish. Both state and federal legislation and regulations must be monitored on a continual, rather than crisis-oriented basis. This would allow input into legislation and regulations as they are being developed rather than only when they are enforced. The Pennsylvania Farmers Association provides ongoing monitoring and lobbying of the developments affecting farmers. Membership in the organization by either the Amish farmers or a liaison to the farmers may be the most effective and efficient way to protect their interest. . . .

There is some urgency to this matter. Many Amish are clearly uninformed about the regulations with which they are expected to comply. A great number of them are presently violating environmental laws and could be issued citations on a daily basis. It is essential that the Amish are provided with copies of the regulations, that they assess the impact of compliance on their way of life, and take steps to either comply or obtain some kind of special exemption. The farmers must also be presented with the technical and legal options for contesting citations issued under the broad parameters of the environmental legislation.

We have arranged a meeting between Amish bishops and the regulatory authorities, to take place on March 2, 1989. Both policy makers and enforcement officers have been invited. Alan Musselman, Lancaster Farmland Trust, is acting as facilitator. Our goal is to educate the Amish as to the regulations that apply to them, to educate the regulators as to Amish culture and to promote a dialogue between the parties regarding cultural and religious beliefs affecting the ability of the Amish to comply with these regulations. Interest in this meeting has been so great that it has been rescheduled to take place in the local fire hall in order to accommodate all the farmers who asked to attend.

James Haggerty, then head of DER, was on hand for the March meeting. By Haggerty's account and that of many there, the meeting cleared the air, helped local authorities and Amish farmers come to understand one another better, and provided a forum for Haggerty to address "arbitrary and unreasonable" enforcement on the part of some sewage officers. A short time later, it was rumored that two county sewage enforcement officers known for rigid, uncompromising enforcement of the law might be fired.

But this was all far, far from Goshen. And Fisher wasn't embroiled over manure: it was his house—and his outhouse.

◆

On March 27, 1989, David Fisher went to Marvin Stoner's office on Black Bear Road in Quarryville. He asked Stoner for a permit for the green, plastic portable outhouse that sat just outside of his still-unoccupied home. Stoner denied the request.

Fisher went home and drafted a letter to Stoner with the assistance of an English friend:

First, let me clearly state my intentions to ensure that everything will be done to keep the waters of the township clear. However, let me also state just as clearly that there are principles of a religious nature involved which prohibit me from taking certain steps which some not having such limitations might be able to take. From this it becomes clear that we must accomplish the legislative intent of Act 537 within both legislative intent *and* religious limitations. I have asked some others in our circles of faith who have more experience in these matters to provide us technical assistance in reaching a proper solution from both of these perspectives.

Let us review our discussion today. . . . We showed you from the very clear DER technical manual used by the state to direct your position, which clearly permitted a privy for on-lot processing of sewage when no pressure water was hooked up to the structure, and when the lot was not a part of a for-profit development, precisely the conditions on our small farm. You told us that "the guidelines don't count," and that we could "with the guidelines and five cents buy a cup of coffee. . . ."

We showed you, from your own DER Technical Manual, how legislative intent clearly excluded concern about small farms, and you dismissed that. We showed you how our religious convictions prohibited us from using technology to produce the pressure water needed to make these systems work, and you dismissed that. You told us that religious grounds could have no effect on any question of sewage treatment. We explained how the same convictions allowed for a similar exclusion in the case of public education, and the same conflict was in place here, which you dismissed. . . .

It has always been traditional on the small farm setting to handle the low level of sewage—especially as in our case where there is no pressurized water—with a privy with holding tank. This is clearly permissible by the guidelines for administration of Act 537.

You see, our whole reason for living what you might call a deprived life, what some call a simple, God-fearing life, is to be obedient to the

Bible in being outside the entanglements of the world system. Those who might choose to live in the luxuries of city life also take upon themselves the responsibility to live the life of building permits, social security systems, drivers licenses, etc. Those who choose to avoid these as sinful are led to accept the farm life, more specifically, the subsistence of self-sufficient farm life, as a distinct way of life. As long as this Godly balance is maintained, God will permit America to exist, just as he did Rome. Our forefathers were burned at the stake rather than accept what to them were unGodly [*sic*] demands of government, and we can certainly do no less. We recognize that there is a need to take care of sewage, but the privy and the tiny amounts of gray water in the garden or compost bin have always been well-sufficient to prevent runoff in our no-pressure water situation, and this clearly meets the intent of the state legislation. . . .

Accordingly, we again request a set of approved plans for a privy, that we may expedite the securing of the appropriate permit.

The next day Stoner wrote back:

I would like to clear up any misunderstanding you may have regarding our meeting of March 27, 1989, in my office.

I stated that it is a violation of Section 7 of the Act of January 24, 1966, PL 1535 Act 537 to construct, or to request bid proposals for construction, or to install or occupy any building or structure for which an individual permit system is to be installed, without first obtaining a permit. I also stated that it is a violation of the same Act 537 to construct or alter an individual sewage system without first obtaining a permit. Also, no structure may be occupied and no sewage system may be used until the Sewage Enforcement Officer gives written approval to cover the system and use it.

As far as a privy is concerned, I cannot give you a permit for a privy to be used at a permanent residence.

First of all, you may not receive a permit for any type of sewage system until you have obtained either a land development plan approval or a subdivision plan approval.

Second, the permit for a privy may not be issued unless Drumore Township has a holding tank ordinance.

Third, all permits for privies and holding tanks may not be issued by the Township Sewage Officer until approval has been granted by DER.

Fourth, and probably most important, a privy does not handle wash water or kitchen water, both of which in Pennsylvania are also sewage and must be disposed of into a septic tank and whatever secondary treatment the soil dictates.

The Sewage Enforcement Office's training manual that you refer to is just what the title says. It was written as a training aid and reference book. . . . The manual is not, and never was, law. If you wish to find out

the Pennsylvania sewage act regulations, I would suggest that you obtain a copy of Act 537 and the chapters related to it and the Clean Streams Law of Pennsylvania.

When a water tank is placed on a hill above the house and water is piped into the home from it, you do have water under pressure. Every two feet of elevation head will give you one pound of water pressure, and regardless of how you interpret that, it is a scientific fact that a standing head of water does create pressure. The sewage regulations were written for all people regardless of religion, color, or creed, to safely dispose of rural waste by soil renovation.

I do hope that we can settle this problem as quickly as possible, but I must remind you that I did not write the law. I strictly enforce the law as it was written.

You must first obtain either a land development plan approval or a subdivision plan approval. Then you must obtain a sewage permit.

If you do any further work on the house, or occupy the house, or install a sewage system without first obtaining a sewage permit, I will be forced to take legal action.

Stoner invoked the letter of the law; Fisher invoked his faith. This was the impasse, with no resolution in sight. It was hard to know what could forestall a collision.

◆

In early April 1989, heedless of Stoner's threats, Fisher finished the three-bedroom house-barn and moved his furniture into it. He and Sarah even stocked up the pantry, but they did not yet occupy the dwelling.

At the same time, Stoner filed complaints against Fisher and his father-in-law, Christian Lapp. The two men were scheduled to appear at separate hearings. Fisher was charged with building a residence without a sewage permit; Lapp was charged because he was the legal owner of the property. Both were found guilty; both paid $100 in fines plus court costs.

Fisher immediately reapplied for a permit and was denied. A certified letter Stoner sent Fisher on April 21, 1989, read, "Basically . . . we may not issue a permit until you have obtained subdivision planning module approval."

But the Lancaster Planning Commission eventually approved Fisher's planning module; Drumore township supervisors received notification from DER, which seemed as if it would clear the way for issuing a permit for Fisher's privy, since as Fisher had written Stoner earlier, DER permitted privy use in other parts of the state.

Again aided by an English friend, Fisher wrote Stoner on May 9, 1989, from the inside of his house-barn, where he and his family were now living. He pointed out that the planning module had been approved. "Given this fact," Fisher declared, "there should be no further procedural barrier standing in the way of our receiving approval of an official permit for our privy.

"We are thus once again making an official request of a permit for our privy. Our children have undergone sickness because of twice daily having to walk the long distance in the rain to the barn to do chores, and further delay in securing the permit now that all the procedural reasons for delay have been solved places their health in unneeded and unreasonable jeopardy."

Again Stoner denied Fisher's request.

In June Fisher asked Stoner to conduct a "perc test," a standard procedure to determine the degree to which a given plot of soil can accommodate liquid waste (including what is known as "gray water"—dishwater and water used for laundry). While on Fisher's property to complete the test, Stoner took the opportunity to inspect the premises.

Stoner noticed a "pipe" that led from the horse stalls up to the second-floor living quarters. For Stoner, it was the straw that broke the camel's back. In his eyes—and according to technicalities of law—Fisher now had water under pressure in his home. The regulations state clearly that a privy or chemical toilet is permissible only "when such use is proposed for a structure on an isolated lot which is not presently served and will not be served by water under pressure." Stoner viewed Fisher's action as a breach of trust and a clear indication of his intention to disobey sewage regulations.

The fact of the matter was that the "pipe" Fisher had installed was a green garden hose that ran down to a small, muddy spring Fisher's boys had dug out below the barn. Using an old gasoline sump pump, Fisher was running water into the barn for the dozen or so horses he was keeping at the time. Twice a day—at morning and evening choring times—he would run the pump long enough to water the horses. But the pump was rickety, and would often sputter and die, reversing the flow of water. Then, Amos, the oldest of Fisher's boys, would have to suck on the end of the hose until the silty water came gushing at his face and the flow was restored.

At first, Fisher used this system only for watering his livestock. For his family's drinking water, he had the boys fill five-gallon plastic buckets at his father-in-law's house up the long hill and tow back the heavy load in a garden cart. But when Fisher found an old stainless-steel bulk milk tank at an auction, he thought of a way to improve the cumbersome arrangement: he placed the huge tank on the second floor of the barn, near the kitchen, and when the family needed water, he would switch the hose from the horse trough below, up to the tank. Now, his wife, Sarah, only had a few feet to walk for cooking and wash water, not the few hundred yards the children had had to walk before.

This was the "pressurized-water" system that Stoner said disqualified Fisher from receiving a permit.

After learning of Stoner's most recent denial, Fisher wrote another letter—this time a terse, direct letter, dated June 23: "This is to let you know that we are willing to put a regular sewage system in if a privy with a holding tank is not legal; we are not willing to go with a system that requires any automatic equipment or pumps. . . . P.S. Please send us a permit."

Again Stoner denied the request:

In response to your letter dated June 23, 1989, which I received July 3, 1989, I cannot change the laws of the Commonwealth of Pennsylvania. The area that you requested me to conduct a soil test on has a percolation rate of 120 min. per 1 inch, which requires an elevated sand mound pressure doseing [sic] system. . . .

You have several choices which you can consider at this time: (1) Install an air system and obtain a permit to install an elevated sand mound at the site tested. (2) You can test an area up on the hill above your house, but this will require the use of a lift pump even if the soil test is better. (3) You can evacuate the house and use it as a barn, which would eliminate the need for a sewage system.

As you know, you have furnished this building with water under pressure. You have constructed and occupied it without first obtaining a sewage permit. You have already been convicted of violating the laws of the Commonwealth of Pennsylvania and you are still in violation.

The letter concluded, "Within ten days of receipt of this letter if you have not obtained a sewage permit, or have not vacated the house I will begin to file charges each day while the violation continues and will use every means possible and available to force you to comply with the laws of the Commonwealth of Pennsylvania."

On July 7th, two days after Stoner wrote back to Fisher, a warrant for the re-arrest of David Fisher was issued by Solanco District Justice Joseph V. Bledsoe—the second time Fisher had been charged with violating the state's sewage facilities law.

In an article in the *Lancaster Intelligencer Journal* dated July 18, 1989, Stoner was quoted as saying that even if Fisher "were to take out the pressurized water from the stable" (which he said he'd do "if that's the only thing holding up the permit") Stoner said he would not issue a privy permit. "The fact that he has water under pressure in the structure indicates his intention. Even if he removed it, there would still be a question of his future intention to bring water into the building."*

The article concluded with Stoner saying he would probably prosecute Fisher one more time "and then we'll go to county court and ask for a court order that he [Fisher] either put in a proper system, or vacate the building." A warrant was again issued on August 7, 1989.

On August 9, 1989, a police car turned off Sawmill Road. It made its way slowly down the long gravel driveway leading to the hollow in which the Fisher's house-barn stood—a wide trail of dust in its wake. The police car stopped directly in front of the house-barn.

Hearing the car's approach, the Fisher children ran to the windows. While they and Sarah watched, David was hauled off to Quarryville in the police car. There he was informed that he would have to appear in the Solanco District Court on September 7, 1989.

◆

I had been watching from a distance as events unfolded for a man whose barn I had helped build. I had also been in contact with

* Woodcock, James A., "Amishman Faces Arrest for Barn-dwelling," *The Lancaster Intelligencer Journal*, July 18, 1989, page B–4.

Elizabeth Place in William Ball's office. We were trying to figure out if there was some sewage system Fisher could install on his property that could effectively handle gray water, appease Stoner, and allow Fisher to stay in line with his religious convictions. I had spent many summer hours on the telephone talking with soil scientists, soil physicists, private soil science consultants, water-quality specialists at DER, and so on. A soil physicist at Penn State University told me, "There are *always* alternatives with this kind of thing."

I had also accompanied Fisher and several other Amishmen to a township meeting (at which Marvin Stoner was also present), stood up, and asked to make a statement for the record. I was asked if I were Fisher's lawyer. I said I was his friend.

I read part of Martin Luther King, Jr.'s "Letter from Birmingham Jail" aloud, the portion making the distinction between a just and an unjust law: "A just law is a man-made code that squares with the moral law or the law of God. An unjust law is a code that is out of harmony with the moral law. To put it in the terms of St. Thomas Aquinas: An unjust law is a human law that is not rooted in eternal law or natural law. Any law that uplifts human personality is just. Any law that degrades human personality is unjust."

On September 6, 1989, I flew to Lancaster with a typewriter and a pile of notes from numerous summer telephone conversations. At the Lancaster airport I was to meet another friend of his, Robert Dicks, who would be waiting to drive to Goshen with me. Dicks had long been a mid-level bureaucrat in state government. He knew the language of regulation well, had left state government, joined an Old Order Mennonite group around Port Treverton, and had been acting for some time as Fisher's self-appointed "counselor."

As Dicks and I drove down Route 222 for southern Lancaster County, he talked nonstop, "briefing me" on what had transpired. I was struck at once by how combative and legalistic this convert to nonresistant Old Order life was, and struck by the assault on the Catholic Church he launched into when, in answer to his pretentious question "What is your belief in our Lord Jesus?" I told him through clenched teeth that I am a Catholic. As we headed for Goshen I had the terrible feeling that I was bringing someone to Fisher's hearing I shouldn't be bringing.

When we arrived and walked into the thoroughly lived-in house-barn, I thought ironically of my conversation with David Fisher when Levi and I had left the barn-raising and Fisher had said, "You'll have to come back when it's all finished."

"That's a promise," I had said. And now, here I was.

Fisher, Dicks, and I stayed up until two o'clock in the morning, drawing up a document for Fisher to read before the judge the next morning. Dicks' retributive statements provoked Fisher. I tried to remind Dicks that it was important for David to show good intention, to stay calm and work with the local officials. This was difficult.

It was important for David to express his concern for the environment, to express and demonstrate his commitment to finding an appropriate system which was consonant with his religious beliefs, to cite a DER document stating that there is no surface or ground water pollution from gray water, but instead *only when gray water is put through a sewage system.* And because Fisher had, under Dicks' tutelage, become something of an expert on DER legalese himself, Fisher wanted to read this passage from the DER Technical Manual: "The extent to which we generate waste water has increased tremendously over the past fifteen years. Many homes are now equipped with automatic washers, garbage grinders, dishwashers, showers, etc., all of which contribute greatly to the amount of waste water that must ultimately be disposed of in a satisfactory manner." The system being detailed to handle such waste operated at a minimum basis of 400 gallons of water.

Fisher would stand before Judge Bledsoe and—once again—explain that he and his family used only thirty-five gallons of water a day. He and Dicks agreed that Dicks would serve as his counsel.

◆

On the morning of the hearing, David mentioned that he had rented a van and would I mind bringing a few of his neighbors to the hearing? I drove around Goshen gathering some of David's friends. As David and I went around to his neighbors', I tried to tell him how wary I was of Dicks' counsel. But David's mind was made up.

133

When we arrived in the courtroom in Quarryville, Stoner was sitting on the left side of the room; Fisher sat on the right. Holding the three-page document we had typed up the night before, Fisher took the stand. His friends watched from the back of the courtroom.

Fisher read haltingly. In addition to making his good intentions known and once again running through DER technicalities, Fisher said that the steps taken by the Sewage Enforcement Officer to enforce his interpretation of the law had been both *arbitrary* and *unreasonable*. In particular, Fisher noted the effects on his family seeing him "taken away in a police car like a common criminal."

Then Robert Dicks stood up. His effect on Judge Bledsoe was immediate. Though the technical points Dicks reviewed sounded good, his manner was completely off-putting. The labyrinth of detail available to Dicks—detail he discussed at great length—was lost on Bledsoe—and me. Bledsoe finally interrupted him and asked him to make concluding statements.

Next, Stoner spoke. He mentioned the water line in the horse stable, the fact that the water line precluded the use of a privy, and DER's denials of Fisher's requests.

Bledsoe turned to Stoner and asked if things couldn't be worked out. Then turning to Fisher he said earnestly with his hands folded in front of him, "Come up with a plan."

I empathized with the judge. To me it seemed that he was as sick of all of this as everybody else. He found Fisher guilty and fined him $300 plus court costs—the third time Fisher had been fined—and gave Fisher sixty days to comply or "come up with something."

On Wednesday, October 25, 1989, David Fisher again appeared in court. For his refusal to pay the fines and his continued use of the green plastic outhouse, Judge Bledsoe ordered that Fisher serve thirty days in the Lancaster County Prison.

Fisher was silent throughout the hearing. There were about thirty Amish people and many English on hand; when court was adjourned, one of the English people requested a moment of silent prayer.* The township police kept everybody in the courtroom until

---

* The Amish honored this request and stood with the rest of the crowd, but in fact they were not praying. Their faith enjoins them to avoid praying in public.

Fisher was put in a police car and driven off to the county prison —the first Lancaster County Amishman jailed since the public-schooling controversies in the 1950s.

That night, David's horses broke loose from their stalls. Sarah, the children, and the neighbors rounded them back up.

On October 31, 1989, Fisher wrote from prison to an English friend, this time, with no assistance:

> I can't explain how precious and important your letter is to me. . . . The care taker don't thing I belong here and are very good to me but still its a strange place. I think I am in the best part of the Jail. What they call the work release part. But still to be with a group of cocain dealers and drinker cigarret smoking cusing + swering seems quite strange. At the same time it is strange how respectful and friendly they are to me so far no one has caused me any trouble whatsoever. It is very sad to see what kind of out look most of these people have of life. A lot of them know each other well they get out of prison for a couple of months then come back in for maybe 12 or 20 month again to meet their buddies (I don't know if you can call it friends as it don't always sound very friendly) . . . And for visiting I am restricked to 4 hr. a week. . . .

The next day, this editorial appeared in the Quarryville paper:

◆

FISHER BELONGS IN JAIL
(Editorial by Fran Maye, Editor, *The Sun Ledger*,
Quarryville, PA, November 1, 1989)

David Fisher belongs in jail.

Fisher, an Amish farmer who lives in Drumore Township, is serving a thirty-day jail term after refusing to pay fines for violating Pennsylvania's Sewage Facilities Act.

Fisher, you see, apparently felt he was above the law when he decided not to obtain a proper sewage permit when he was building facilities in the upper deck of his barn. According to state law, outhouses can be used only in areas where there is no pressurized water system available for conventional toilets.

Fisher felt it was within his right to use an outhouse instead of modern sewage facilities. After all, it's his property, and he can do with it as he sees fit, right?

135

Wrong.

Some people may not agree with all of the laws—the local laws, the county laws, the state laws, and the national laws—but they're for the overall good of the people. Lights are required on buggies for the overall good of the people. Subdivision laws exist to protect the interest of most people. Of course, if we didn't have these laws, some Amish could be producing milk that isn't pasteurized.*

Nobody's singling out Fisher. He had his chances. His request went through the judicial process, and it was denied. He was given several opportunities to pay his fine.

We shouldn't feel sorry for him just because he is Amish and maybe doesn't have the money to pay the fine. He received due process of the law just like you and I had we been in the same situation. In fact, it's reassuring when you see a judicial process that doesn't play favorites. Enforce the law the same for everyone.

After Fisher's sentencing, many of his Amish friends stood outside District Justice Joseph Bledsoe's office praying out loud for him.† It's too bad many of the Amish feel the judicial system is slighted against them. Laws are established for the protection and welfare of all residents.

Some laws may not be the best, but that's the great thing about democracy. We have the power to put pressure on lawmakers to help change them. In this case, however, the laws don't need changed [sic]; someone needs to give David Fisher a lesson in Political Science 101.

◆

* In fact, *all* milk produced in Lancaster County—on Amish and non-Amish dairy farms alike—is produced unpasteurized. At the point of sale, that is, at the point at which milk is taken from the dairy farm's cooling tank and then transported by truck to a production plant, it is unpasteurized. Pasteurization (the heating of milk to a certain temperature in order to kill bacteria) occurs at the production plant. As an Amish friend of mine said, "We haven't quite figured out a way for our cows to pasteurize their own milk yet." Furthermore, according to Carol Wallace, Lab Evaluator for Milk Sanitation, Pennsylvania Department of Agriculture, Bureau of Foods and Chemistry, Division of Milk Sanitation, it is perfectly legal in Pennsylvania to sell raw milk (milk that isn't pasteurized) if the dairy is inspected twice a month by a state milk sanitarian. Maye's editorial, on this and another key point, reflects his misunderstanding of Amish life and custom.

† This is not, in fact, accurate. See p. 134.

Sixteen days into his sentence, as a result of a motion filed stating that Fisher had not been given thirty days to appeal his jail sentence, Fisher was released from prison. But the battle between Stoner and Fisher was endless. The fines continued. Fisher sought the advice of another self-proclaimed counselor, Sydney Moyers, a man Judge Bledsoe would eventually have dragged out of his courtroom for refusal to leave when ordered to do so. It is rumored that an Amish elder finally paid Fisher's fines. Fisher and his family abandoned their house-barn in late 1990. They moved out of Lancaster County and now live in a rented house in the western part of the state.

◆

In January of 1992, the Quarryville *Sun Ledger* reported that twelve Amish families were planning to move out of southern Lancaster County and start a new settlement in Indiana. "We used to think of [this area] as a nice area," an Amishman was quoted as saying, "but in the last ten years traffic has doubled and the zoning laws are against us."* Some of these families were David Fisher's neighbors.

*Maye, Fran, "Amish Families Moving Out of Solanco," *The Sun Ledger:* Quarryville, Pa., January 8, 1992, page 1.

PART EIGHTEEN

If this had been done by an enemy I could bear his taunts. If
a rival had risen against me, I could hide from him.

But it is you, my own companion, my intimate
friend! How close was the friendship
between us. We walked together in
harmony in the house of God.
—Psalm 55, 13–15

◆

*For all the ugliness of the June 19th meeting and what it portends,
I will never forget the moment when Gideon Fisher took hold of
his hat and stood. Those present with the eyes to see it suddenly
beheld something. Something blinding. Something beyond doubt,'
something affirming, something of God. Not the facts of a predica-
ment, or the truth.*
    But Truth.

◆

On April 23, 1990, the *Lancaster New Era* reported that the Lancaster Planning Commission was considering a proposal by Amos S.
Stoltzfus, a restauranteur/meat store operator, to develop eighty-one
acres of his farmland, lying about a third of a mile east of the village of Intercourse. The proposed project, known as "the Meadows,"

would include ninety-eight houses and four commercial buildings. The proposal had not materialized overnight; in fact, Stoltzfus had been laying the groundwork for years. In 1972 he had quietly rezoned most of the acreage from rural to residential. In the summer of 1986 almost half the land was rezoned again from residential and rural to commercial. Then, in November of 1989, almost twenty-two acres were rezoned from rural to residential. Stoltzfus's Amish neighbors had privately wondered for years "when the bulldozers are coming."

Nor was this the first the public had heard of Stoltzfus's plans to develop the property. Stoltzfus had announced in 1988 that he wanted to build a retirement community consisting of seventy single-family dwellings and five hundred other units on the land. Ostensibly, the project would be beneficial to the congregation to which Stoltzfus and his family belonged, Ridgeview Mennonite Church, housed a mile away in a modern brick structure, overlooking one of the most spectacular rural vistas in Lancaster County.

Saddened by Stoltzfus's plans for his property, residents of Leacock Township nonetheless consoled themselves with the knowledge that "at least it's for the old folks," as some Amish said. When news announcing the change in plan hit the Lancaster papers, local people were stunned. Stoltzfus himself offered no public explanation.

Rumors flew around Leacock Township: none of Amos Stoltzfus's three sons wanted to farm anymore; a development would make the whole family rich quick and permanently remove the obligation of the farm from its hands; there was more money to be made from a development than a retirement community, and the ninety-eight houses would sell for $150,000 each; the streets in the development would be named for the five Stoltzfus children, three sons and two daughters, etc.

The Lancaster Planning Commission urged Leacock Township officials to examine the impact of the project on the village of Intercourse. Nonetheless, the Commission approved the plan, provided that nineteen "conditions" be met.

On May 2nd a letter by John Hostetler appeared on the editorial pages of the *Lancaster New Era*. Hostetler's chief concerns were the impact of "the Meadows" on Leacock Township's farming community and the propriety of the relationship between the Stoltzfuses and the Township Supervisors.

"To live in Lancaster County," Hostetler's letter began, "one must be prepared to have a broken heart. That is, if one cares about the landscape.

In the past four years, everyone has defined "growth" in their own way. The term is not all that difficult. Growth and tranquility belong together. One without the other turns into perversion.

We are living in a county out of balance. While we sleep the urban planners in Miami and San Francisco make plans for shopping centers in our landscape. They bring them to our local banks for approval and promotion.

Growth has overtaken tranquility in this place. Excessive, inordinate, and rapacious love of money has the upper hand. How can we teach the proponents of growth the value of tranquility? Tranquility means rest, freedom from agitation, and from addiction.

The most fertile soil in the whole world is being taken out of production by housing developments which tarnish the character of this region. A curious example of this is the proposal of Amos S. Stoltzfus and his family to build ninety-eight houses on their farm adjacent to Intercourse. A friend recently called it morally repugnant.

The project will have severe negative impacts on nearby farmlands. It is not just the land that is at stake, but the legacy of hundreds of years of farming experience. This is part of William Penn's "holy experiment."

Were the supervisors of Leacock Township sleeping when they voted to allow agricultural lands to be used for residential development? Since the son of Mr. Stoltzfus (J. Myron) is chairman of the township supervisors, are we to understand that he has had no participation in the change of zoning? Would the same board have approached such a change for other farmers in the neighborhood?

There are of course constitutional rights to travel or to seek a dream house of one's liking. But such rights do have limits. Of course, people have to have a place to live. But we are not allowed to have houses in our national parks. Lancaster's landscape is the equivalent of the Grand Canyon or the California redwoods.

This area has all the scenic beauty of a park. It needs no fence. There are no laws forbidding owners to treat their land as a park. We need no laws until there is a desecration of the common good. But then it's often too late.

We have an opportunity. An opportunity to learn how humans can live in harmony with nature, and at peace with cultural diversity.

But what of Amos Stoltzfus, his wife, Mary, and their five children? Do they understand the awesome consequences of their decision?

There must be a better way. If we lose our farms, we will have lost the soul of our nation. There are many Stoltzfuses and I expect most are unaware of other alternatives. The Bible supports a moral economy, but not an exploitive one.

Mr. Stoltzfus, what you do will set a very powerful example. You can leave behind a monument of desecration. Or you can preserve a landmark of loving stewardship which defies the price tag.

An editor's note appeared under the piece noting that at the time the Leacock Township Supervisors rezoned the Stoltzfus tract, J. Myron abstained from voting.

In calling on the Stoltzfus family to weigh the effects of its actions, Hostetler was also enjoining them to recall their Amish upbringing: Amos and Mary Stoltzfus had been raised in the Old Order Amish church, but as a young man Amos had been excommunicated for buying an automobile. Although Stoltzfus had left the Amish community long ago, his farm still sat smack in its midst. If "the Meadows" was built, the differences between Amos Stoltzfus and the community he left would be permanently etched on the landscape.

Hostetler's editorial crystallized deep sentiments about the proposed development—both for and against—sentiments that also struck at the root of familial ties across generations, changing views of vocation as well as what has been called "rightful land use."

On May 5th, Mary Stoltzfus, Amos's wife, wrote to Hostetler. Her letter recalled ties of faith and blood between her family and Hostetler's, ties which she felt made Hostetler's public criticism of "the Meadows" a personal attack on her family.

"First of all," Mary Stoltzfus complained bitterly, "we are not the kind of people who like to see our name in print. It is this kind of action that causes one to lose respect, and I have lost a lot of respect for you. You were greatly in error to mention my name and the name of our son, J. Myron. He is the chairman of the board of supervisors of Leacock Township, but did you fail to read the editor's note following your letter?

I personally feel you owe J. Myron a public apology for this injustice. J. Myron nor myself [sic] have anything to do with this project nor do any of our five children. So please, John, do not use our name in the paper again.

Where did you get your information? You seem to know us well and

141

where we live. Why did you not come personally and we would have been glad to give you our time to air your concerns.

Why is this such a concern of yours? To my knowledge you have never lived in our area. Is it to protect the Amish? Your roots and mine? If so, they can usually take care of their own issues. Why did you use the news media to do your mud-slinging?

I can't believe Jesus would use this method of dealing with his fellowman [*sic*]. The Lord has been good to us. He has blessed us abundantly, all that we are and ever hope to be we owe to God almighty but He has also blessed us with a desire for hard work. Amos and I worked very hard on that farm. Things were not handed to us on a silver spoon.

Let us be careful we do not worship the creation (this includes Lancaster County farmland) instead of the Creator.

John, please let us not revert back to the character of your father and my grandmother, who were brother and sister, and, sad to say, enemies in almost all of their adult life. Let us rise and live above that.

I am thankful that my father, Isaac Huyard (you knew him well), taught us a better way. By word and example, by love and forgiveness. And most of all, he taught us the way in knowing Jesus as our Lord and Savior.

Forgiveness is a choice, and not a feeling (if it were a feeling I couldn't do it) but I chose to forgive you.

I close with a quote from A. Don Augsburger. "Forgiveness is the aroma of the flower when it is crushed."

Hostetler wrote an apology to Mary Stoltzfus for not coming to see her family in person, but stood firm on the rest of his editorial: " 'The Meadows' affects the whole community and is therefore a public issue. . . . To remain silent, is for me to be disobedient to God. . . . If 'your' farm will be transformed into ninety-four houses, I shall have a broken heart."

◆

To understand the depth of sentiment about this issue, the proposed development of "the Meadows" must be seen in the context of the entire county: it is not just one farm being lost, it is one of many more.

From 1970 to 1987 the County's population climbed from 320,000 to 403,700. Its growth rate from 1980 to 1987 was 11.4 percent, compared to a statewide growth rate of 0.6 percent. During the same period, Lancaster County added 41,354 persons, *amounting to 58 percent of the growth of the entire state.* It was the only metropolitan area in Pennsylvania to experience a double-digit growth rate. As of 1984, the county had become the ninetieth largest metropolitan area in the country (Lancaster County comprises a single metropolitan area).*

Here are the figures *Lancaster New Era* reporter Ed Klimuska meticulously compiled illustrating the transformation of Lancaster County: In 1959, 482,579 acres of the county was farmland. In 1987, that figure had dropped to 413,610 acres. This dramatic decline is a direct result of population growth during that period and the resulting pressure for increased development. In 1986 and 1987 alone, 15,000 acres of land were approved for development, and over seven thousand new homes were built. In 1988, five thousand new homes were started.† The figure is often quoted that Lancaster County loses twenty-one acres of farmland to development each day. Today, this trend continues; Lancaster County continues to be a "good" place for inexpensive tract housing, for families purchasing their first homes, and for people from the New York, New Jersey, Delaware, and Baltimore areas. (Higher-priced housing, however, has not traditionally sold well in Lancaster County.)

During the early 1970s when many non-Amish farmers abandoned their farms in southern Lancaster County, the tracts of land were quickly bought up by the Amish, who eagerly brought them back into production. What has changed is that now most non-Amish farmers are selling to developers. Farmland is a diminishing resource, and a burgeoning Amish population has nowhere in the county for its young people to farm. For young Amishmen and women wishing to remain in the county, the pursuit of more worldly occupations is becoming an economic necessity.

Even farms remaining in farming have become vastly more expensive. In December 1988, for example, a sixty-six acre beef and hog farm kept by a county family since 1861 was sold at a public auction for $930,000, or $14,000 an acre, to date a benchmark price for county farmland remaining in farming.

Lancaster County Firsts and Bests, collected by Gerald S. Lestz (Lancaster: John Baer's Sons, 1989), pp. 4–5.

† Klimuska, Ed, "Lancaster County: The (Ex?) Garden Spot of America," Lancaster, Pa.: *The Lancaster New Era*, Reprint, July 1988.

Amish farmers are also keenly aware of the value of their land. For the price of the home farm in Lancaster County, they know they could buy several farms for their children elsewhere. In light of this fact, one Amish elder told me point blank that the amount of scouting activity in 1991 has been without precedent. He said, "The Amish are always looking at land, but this is different. It's happening everywhere; people aren't just talking about it. In 1991, at least twenty families left Lancaster County. In the next few years you're going to see between fifty and a hundred families a year moving away." Today the Amish are combing the Finger Lakes region in New York State, Indiana, the dairy region of Wisconsin, western Ohio, Tennessee, Kentucky, and other areas. And while moving out may be economically viable, psychically the cost of "pulling up deep, strong roots," is great.

I once sat at a luncheon with a Lancaster developer active in the Quarryville area. He said, "If I knew that I could put all my sons on farms by selling the home farm in Lancaster County, I'd sure have to think about that."

I replied, "That's because you and I couldn't possibly imagine what it would mean to be born in the same farmhouse that our fathers and grandfathers were born in. We think what is of 'value' can only be measured in dollars."

The underlying question raised by the plight of the Stoltzfus farm is this: does an individual's constitutional right to do as he or she pleases with personal landholdings override the maintenance of a community's predominant character?

The Amish answer this question "nay."

For some others, like Amos Stoltzfus, the answer is "yes"—but a highly qualified, highly subjective "yes." Here are some examples of those qualifications.

A pizza-parlor operator in Intercourse wanted to obtain a liquor license for his establishment. He was denied—swiftly and resoundingly. The Leacock Township Board of Supervisors and residents expressed concern that one liquor outlet would wreak havoc on the quiet village, especially among young people.

A proposal was also made in Paradise Township for an establishment for "parlor" betting. Upset residents packed the local township meeting and the proposal went down in flames.

When, closer to the city of Lancaster, an entrepreneur announced that he wanted to offer tourists helicopter rides over county farmland, area residents again turned out to voice opposition. The Amish said they were fearful that the swooping, noisy machines would spook their cattle; the entrepreneur rolled up his plans and went home.

So there is a willingness and indeed often an imperative for regarding the moral implications of township issues; there *are* times when individuals' rights are overridden for a common good, especially when community character is at stake.

But land strikes the heart. And the pocketbook.

The question of rightful land use is cast in three different frameworks: political, economic, and religious, as demonstrated in the exchange between John Hostetler and Mary Stoltzfus. In Lancaster County, combinations of the three manifest themselves in two diametrically opposed ethics.

The first defines rightful land use economically and politically. It sees growth as vital to a thriving economy, and home-owning as a fundamental American right. This ethic was recently espoused by the Vice-President of the Building Industry Association of Lancaster County, Scott Jackson:

The constitution of this land allows for certain inalienable rights, among those being the opportunity to bear children and raise a family, to have free access to move around the country at will and reside in any location we so choose, to purchase property freely and to be allowed to maintain and use it as we see fit within the strictures of governing law. . . .

Our expanding economy cannot be halted, for such attempts would indelibly ruin [the] fabric of our community. Continued forward progress is essential in order to maintain the vitality this community enjoys. . . .

We cannot allow any alternative course but this: Lancaster County must and will prosper, all of us have a great stake in this." *

The second ethic involves the notion of land stewardship, that

* Jackson, Scott, "Letters by the People of Lancaster County," in *Living Graciously in Lancaster County*, Lancaster, Pa.: Brookshire Publications, Volume 2, Number 5, January/February 1989, pages 18–19.

people are caretakers of land belonging to God. It was elaborated by an Amishman in a recent edition of an Amish periodical:

[Tourists] take a special interest in the countryside, giving the Amish a lot of credit for its beauty. However, they don't realize that the Lord made the rolling hills and gave the fertile soil, the sunshine and the rain. He gave us the seed to plant that is germinated. No person in the world is able to germinate a grain of seed. Neither can they make a blade of grass grow and reproduce. We can cultivate the soil, plant and harvest, but we have no power to make a plant grow. So there is no honor to the human race for this beautiful countryside.

We live on the land like renters.

After this generation passes on, the land is left behind for another generation to live on.

In defense of his right to sell his farm, an English farmer accused of being a land speculator took the idea of land stewardship to task. "The land may be the Lord's," he said, "but I'm the one who pays the mortgage."

Somewhere in between these two ethical polarities are individuals espousing "managed growth." Advocates of managed growth argue for careful zoning such as that recently enacted in parts of southern Lancaster County, where one acre of land is permissible for housing if twenty-five acres of farmland remain in farming. The trend toward adoption of such zoning is slow and fraught with local political baggage. The Lancaster Planning Commission has developed a Comprehensive Plan for the County, but the commission has very little actual power. It is more an advisory group, and approval of the Comprehensive Plan is subject to the approval of each of Lancaster County's sixty local municipalities, some of which are composed of developers or those in development-related industries.

Some have argued for consolidation of Lancaster County's townships. But even the *idea* of consolidating under "home rule" is repugnant to a population proud of its local identity and control of its own affairs, a population zealously boastful of being "native" to Lancaster County.

◆

Each morning, twenty-seven-year-old Frank Reedy leaves home in Vorhees, New Jersey, drives his car to Philadelphia's 30th Street Station, and boards AMTRAK's 6:45 A.M. Harrisburg-bound train for the hour-and-fifteen-minute-long ride to Lancaster. Reedy works for Armstrong World Industries, a manufacturer of flooring based there. Reedy, his wife (a Lancaster County native from Quarryville), and their fourteen-month-old daughter, like many young families, plan on moving into Lancaster County—where it is realistically possible for them to own their own home. Reedy says the move would be part of "a career path." He also thinks Lancaster County is "an outstanding place to raise a family. It's charming."

When asked if he is worried that if too many people like him move into the County the "charm" will be lost, Reedy replies, "Yes. They've got to control growth; they've got to set rules and abide by them; they've got to make decisions to make sure it doesn't become like Chester County."

"Who is 'they'?" I ask.

"The government," he replies.

◆

In May 1990, the Leacock Township Board of Supervisors announced it would hold a public hearing on June 19th, at which time residents could voice their concerns before the Board voted its final decision on the Stoltzfus project.

This was an important opportunity: surely, if township residents appeared in numbers and aired their concerns, the houses might not get built. While scrambling to finish my dissertation in Cambridge so that I could receive my diploma on June 7th, I wondered how the proposal could be blocked.

Several friends and I decided to publicize Stoltzfus's proposal so the June 19th hearing would be packed. We planned to hold a vigil on the Stoltzfus property, one emphasizing the religious implications of "the Meadows" proposal, and to collect signatures in opposition to the proposed development from tourists—people who had traveled some distance to visit Lancaster County—in order to underscore the national significance of the area. We set a date for the vigil, I called two television stations, and they agreed to be on hand.

147

In late May I took the subway to Chinatown and bought a large piece of burlap and numerous squares of colored felt. I spent an afternoon on the floor of my apartment cutting out felt letters and gluing them onto the burlap for a banner six feet wide by four feet tall.

I drove with my Boston friends to Lancaster County, where we met up with two other friends, "native" Lancastrians. The next day, the first Saturday in June, armed with three hundred xeroxed leaflets, the burlap banner, a banjo, and a songbook, we headed for Amos Stoltzfus's farm just outside the village of Intercourse.

When we pulled into the parking lot of Kitchen Kettle Village at ten A.M. it was already packed with cars and campers. We walked down Route 772, to the edge of the Stoltzfus property. We climbed up the embankment, and unfurled the burlap banner.

THE LAND SHALL NOT BE BOUGHT AND SOLD FOREVER
FOR THE LAND IS MINE   —LEVITICUS

Two camera crews arrived. We sang "This Land Is Your Land" and other songs while passing out leaflets to the cars willing to slow down and take them from us.

We decided to be more confrontational, so we took the banner directly to the front of the entrance to the Stoltzfus Farm Restaurant and leafletted the many tourists now arriving for lunch. Several waitresses and busboys peered curiously out at us from the windows.

We said to tourists, "The owner of this property wants to turn the land you see into ninety-eight houses. Help save Lancaster County farmland. Don't eat here today." The leaflet had J. Myron Stoltzfus's address on it. We urged people to write him and make their opposition known.

Suddenly, Ken Stoltzfus, one of the three Stoltzfus sons, came outside. He walked right up to me; his jaw was set.

The cameras whirred.

Ken Stoltzfus stuck his face in mine and said in a tense voice, "I've come out here in a spirit of loving forgiveness to ask you to leave our property."

"I can't do that," I said nervously.

"Why are you doing this?" Stoltzfus asked. The artificial piety left his voice. "This property was rezoned a long time ago. What Dad's doing is legal."

"It may be legal but it isn't moral," I said.

"And what are you people doing here? You're not from around here. Where *are* you from?"

"From Boston," we said.

"Outsiders."

"We're not leaving," I said. "You'll need to call the police. We're here because we think what your family is about to do is wrong."

Ken Stoltzfus pointed at the banner. "That's a Jewish quotation," he said. "You people are living in Old Testament times."

"I thought all of the Bible was meant to be paid attention to," I said. "Not just the parts you agreed with."

He stood looking at me for a long time.

I was suddenly fearful.

Finally Ken Stoltzfus got into a Ford Bronco-type vehicle, revved up the engine, and then tore down the restaurant parking lot, turning onto Route 772. He peeled down the road, flying past a buggy. We stood singing "Little Boxes" and passing out leaflets for another hour or so. The camera crews packed up and left.

We walked back to Kitchen Kettle Village and collected signatures from tourists, many of whom were older people visiting Lancaster County because they had been born and raised on farms themselves and had come to recall those days as they looked at the farms here. They eagerly signed our petitions. Listening to their stories, I felt ashamed of some of my misconceptions about tourists. Many of the stories we heard as we collected signatures were very moving. An elderly woman from Wisconsin who had been raised on a dairy farm said, "I can't explain it; it's just good to see that people are still living like this. I wish I still was."

Other tourists said they had visited a few years ago and were shocked to see how built up and commercialized Lancaster County had become since their last visit. One man said, "In twenty years there probably won't be any small farms left in America, so I'm showing them to my kids while they're still around."

The third group we spoke to was composed of educated, rather well-off people in their early thirties. Mostly they were touring the countryside riding expensive bicycles and wearing brightly colored spandex outfits. They categorically refused to sign the petitions. I thought of the man in red riding the yellow bicycle through Valley Forge National Park.

All in all, we collected over 150 signatures in less than an hour. The names we collected were from all over the United States and Canada. But I still had doubts. How could we convince someone like Amos Stoltzfus that Lancaster County's farmland was a national treasure? And who were we to even attempt to convince him? We were not farmers; we were a group of (so-called) intellectuals. On what moral ground were we standing, to presume to tell a farmer what was "best" for his land?

On Sunday we drove back to Boston. I received my diploma Thursday morning. My family left late Thursday afternoon; that night I went to Fenway Park on the T with six friends from the Graduate School of Education to see the Red Sox play the Yankees. We sat in the bleachers drinking watery beer. I worried about the Stoltzfus farm throughout the entire game.

Several days later friends called to say that the Amish were circulating a petition among themselves stating their opposition to "the Meadows." I said I would try and come down the weekend before the Tuesday, June 19th hearing. I wondered if the Amishmen collecting signatures might be glad for an English driver to take them around. Other friends called to say a number of television and newspaper reporters had called; they had seen our vigil on television and wanted to know more about what was occuring in Leacock Township and what might happen at the June 19th hearing. Their main question was, "Would the Amish be at the meeting?"

I flew to Lancaster from Boston on June 16th and then drove to Paradise to see Elam's family. Levi was very interested in the work we were doing concerning "the Meadows." He also said that if the Amish petition had come his way he probably wouldn't sign it. "I'd hate to see those houses going up, but I just don't think it's a good idea to get involved in this sort of thing."

I replied saying that everything in *my* upbringing taught me that if you worked earnestly within the political system, things would change.

Levi looked at me and said, "My granddad used to say that given the choice between twelve men at the voting booth or one man on his knees before God, he'd take the man on his knees any day of the week."

On Monday, June 18th, I paid a call on one of the Amish elders circulating the petitions. He would be very grateful for a ride, he said. A little while later I came back to his farm with a car and we drove around for three hours.

We went to small shops and farms throughout Leacock Township. I sat in the car while the elder got out and spoke with his brethren. Many Amishmen eagerly signed the petition. Some refused, saying so, in Dutch, in no uncertain terms. It was moving and sad to see this very old man making his way through his people on behalf of something he would surely prefer to have nothing to do with.

The petition read:

We the undersigned are shaken by the proposed development called Meadows at Intercourse which would allow 98 houses to be built on the 81 acres owned by Amos S. Stoltzfus. We ask that it be disallowed.

The project would destroy forever the 84 [sic] acres for farming.

The introduction of a housing development is an invasion of the natural landscape and character of the area.

The project would have great economic impact on other farms in the area.

There would be great incentive for the development of many other acreages in the area.

We are mindful of the necessity of housing for mankind. But there are other acreages that cannot be farmed that would be suitable for housing.

The proposal is a very bad choice for the use of the land.

Our county is blessed with the most productive and fertile soil in the state, even in all of North America, and perhaps in the world.

Without your help our small scale agriculture cannot be maintained.

We beg you to leave the farming lands zoned for agriculture.

At 6:00 P.M., Tuesday, June 19th, I drove from Elam and Rachel's farm in Paradise Township to visit an elderly Amishman named Gideon Fisher, who had been carefully watching the recent unfolding of events in Leacock Township. The last time I'd seen Fisher he had mentioned he would be grateful for a ride to the meeting. We drove to the township building, an oversized garage labeled LEACOCK TOWNSHIP MUNICIPAL BUILDING. It sits just outside of Intercourse, along Route 340, headed toward Lancaster.

Fisher and I were the first ones to show up for the seven o'clock meeting. I had a piece of paper in my pocket with the names of the Township Supervisors on it; I was anxious to meet them.

A white car with the words CLARK AND ASSOCIATES along its side pulled up. The large, middle-aged woman driving it was holding a hoagie sandwich in one hand and the receiver of a car phone with the other, driving the car with one elbow as she bit into the sandwich. She got out of the car, fumbled with a fat set of keys, and unlocked the township building. This was Donna Clark, one of five Township Supervisors.

I walked up to her and said, "Hello. I'm Randy Testa. I—"

"—Yeah, I know who you are, I watch television," she snapped. "That was a dumb stunt you pulled on Amos's property. Now, if you'll excuse me, I'd like to finish the rest of my dinner." Donna Clark went inside the township building, slammed the door, and locked it behind her.

I was dumbfounded. Why would an elected official be offended by my participation in the vigil?

Out of the blue, a helicopter landed in the field adjacent to the township building and a reporter from a Philadelphia television station climbed out! As quickly as she stepped out, a van loaded with men and television cameras pulled up. They were all from the same television station. The reporter said she'd been born and raised in Lancaster County and was very anxious to cover the story of the Stoltzfus property hearing. She asked Fisher if she could speak with him on camera. Politely he said no. The reporter thanked him and left him alone. She asked me to point out the direction of the Stoltzfus property; she and her crew were going to swoop over the farm to take aerial shots before covering the hearing.

Buggies and cars began pulling into the parking lot. Donna Clark unlocked the township building and took her place at one of the seats behind a long table at the front of the room. She continued to eat her sandwich.

Frank and June Hoover, longtime residents of Leacock Township whose property lies adjacent to the Stoltzfus farm, arrived. Frank Hoover had petitions against "the Meadows," with the signatures of over 150 non-Amish township residents, in his possession. Hoover had served on the Board of Supervisors and knows its inner workings well. For the month prior to the hearing, the Hoovers had posted a special message on the billboard in front of their paint store: IMPORTANT TOWNSHIP MEETING JUNE 19, 7:00 P.M. June Hoover, a soft-spoken, religious woman, sat next to her husband wringing her hands throughout the meeting.

The Amishmen with property behind the Stoltzfus farm arrived. They looked somber. Reporters from the Lancaster newspapers arrived. A reporter from the *Philadelphia Inquirer* pulled up with a cameraman. Then others: Richard and Penny Armstrong, John Hostetler, local physician Holmes Morton, Fred Daum of the Lancaster Alliance for New Directions (LAND), more television crews, many more Amish and English township residents, and even a reporter from a London newspaper who had flown from his bureau office in Washington, D.C., to Baltimore and then driven to Leacock Township.

Just before 7:00 P.M. the rest of the Township Supervisors arrived: Jake Smucker, Frank Howe, and Bob Alexander. (The fifth Supervisor, J. Myron Stoltzfus, had removed himself from the proceedings.) As they nervously sat down, the man next to me, a township resident, whispered pointing to the front of the room, "If this proposal goes through, guess who else is gonna get rich?"

Next to arrive were Amos Stoltzfus, flanked by his three sons: Ike, the oldest, who has distanced himself somewhat from his family's entrepreneurial aspirations; J. Myron; and Ken, the youngest. Entering with the family were Stoltzfus's lawyer Donald LeFever, a consultant, and an engineer. Harold Hess also arrived. A local prodevelopment political "boss," he had long ago sold his own farm for development, as Stoltzfus was now hoping to do.

All in all there were over one hundred and fifty people crowded into the airless building, about fifty Amish, a hundred or so English —and about twenty people from the media. The air was so thick with humidity, the smell of perspiration, and tension that somebody opened the rear garage door of the building. Sounds of car and buggy traffic whizzed by all evening. The Amish stayed in the back or leaned on the red fire engine parked on the left side of the garage. Amos's sons sat tensely in the crowd, leaning forward in metal folding chairs. Donna Clark pointed me out to the other

Supervisors, while camera crews filmed everything. The Supervisors looked addled. Clearly, they hadn't anticipated such a turnout, and such a publicized turnout at that. As they regarded the assemblage, they could barely contain their disdain.

Two men representing Amos Stoltzfus's group spoke first. The Supervisors said things to them like "Take as much time as you need," and addressed them with great respect. Watching this, it seemed that we were not at a hearing, but a grand opening. It was also difficult to comprehend the long monologue of technical information they were delivering. When they finished, people in the audience looked numb. I thought the top of my head was going to come off.

Next followed another long, numbing monologue from another consultant. He concluded by saying that when developments are planned, the standard figure used to assess impact on local roads is ten trips per car per day in and out of a development, for each home built. The engineer said if "the Meadows" were built at a figure of approximately one hundred houses, one could count on a *minimum* of a thousand car trips per day in and out of the development onto Route 772—this on an already far-too-busy rural road which many Amish use when they go into Intercourse. The blandness of his voice and the fact that as a *proponent* of the development he would mention such an arresting figure was horrifying and fascinating.

After this, the Board of Supervisors nervously announced that it was going to open the floor to people so they could express their opinions of the project. They asked that township residents speak first, and then, if there was any time left, the floor would be turned over to others wishing to speak. The Supervisors put a time limit on the meeting—it would be over at 9:00 P.M. It was already seven thirty.

Frank Hoover stood up and handed forward the one hundred-plus signatures he had collected from non-Amish residents of the township. I passed our petitions to him and those too went to the front of the room. The Amish passed their own one hundred and fifty signatures forward.

While so many pieces of paper made their way to the Supervisors, it was very quiet. Buggy traffic from Route 340 punctuated

155

the silence. Frank Howe said, "We'll have to look these over carefully," then he shoved the piles of signatures off to one side of the table in front of him.

Hoover then turned to the gathering and said in a quiet voice, "Will all those opposed to 'the Meadows' please rise?" The metal folding chairs squeaked and everyone stood up—everyone, that is, except the Supervisors, Harold Hess, and Amos Stoltzfus's three sons.

Then everyone sat down.

Richard Armstrong called out, "Will all those in *favor* of the proposal please stand?" There was a pause. No one stood up. Not even Amos Stoltzfus. This drew laughter from the gathering.

The Supervisors admonished the crowd and spoke about the importance of "controlled growth" in Lancaster County. Supervisor Jake Smucker pointed out that about fifty acres of *Amish* farmland in Leacock Township had gone from farming into development for small shops over the past year. At this, the audience grumbled loudly: Smucker's comparison of what the Amish were doing in order to stay on their land with what Amos Stoltzfus was proposing in order to make money off of his was both stupid and antagonistic.

A man turned to the gathering and asked, "Do you think *any* of those rich people from New York and New Jersey paying $150,000 for a home are going to join the local fire department? The answer is no! We'll have to upgrade the fire department. And guess who'll pay for that? The answer is you and I will pay for it out of our taxes!" People applauded.

Several mothers stood up and talked about the already-dangerous Route 772. They said they feared for their children, who had to cross the road in order to attend the local elementary school. "What 1,000 more cars will do I'm afraid to imagine," one mother said. Then a young Amishman named Levi stood up and said, "If anybody thinks 772 isn't crowded already, I'd like to take them for a ride to Gap in my buggy. We might make it and we just might not!" Again the crowd stirred.

Standing at the back of the room, Richard Armstrong called to the Board, "Is it your assessment that most of the people here are for Amos's development, or against it?" The Supervisors did not answer the question. Reminiscent of his actions at the Route 30 bypass hearings, Armstrong repeated his question, this time more emphatically. The Supervisors did not answer him. One Supervisor berated the audience for its too-late response to the project.

From the back of the garage I blurted out, "Why are you people *defending* this proposal? This is supposed to be a hearing. But you've already made up your minds! They don't understand, folks, so let's try it again: Will all those opposed to 'the Meadows' please stand?"

People laughed and stood up again.

"There! How many times are we going to have to stand up for you to understand: no one wants this thing built!"

Harold Hess, seated in the audience, stood up and walked to the front of the room, saying as he hitched up his pants, "I think that most of this commotion has to do with outsiders who are stirring the local people up!" There was an awkward silence and he strolled back to his seat.

No one knew what would happen next. The antagonism between the Board and the gathering was pronounced. Suddenly, Gideon Fisher stood up, fumbled with his hat, and then spoke slowly and clearly. Cameras clicked, reporters perked up, and the television camera spotlights aimed right at him.

◆

Excerpts from:

FEARING FOR WAY OF LIFE, AMISH FIGHT SUBDIVISION
(by Paul Nussbaum, staff writer, *Philadelphia Inquirer*, June 21, 1990)

Gideon Fisher, a white-bearded Amish farmer, broke the silence of a lifetime when he stood to speak.

He had come to the township meeting just to listen, because his religious beliefs discouraged anything that might smack of publicity-seeking or self-aggrandizement. For two hours, he sat in the back of the Leacock Township garage that served as a makeshift meeting hall, listening to his neighbors debate the merits of a proposed housing development on Amos Stoltzfus' farm.

The discussion was punctuated by the familiar nighttime highway sounds that drifted in over the shoulders of those who stood three-deep in the open doorway: the whir of passenger cars contrasting with the clip of horses' hooves on the pavement.

Finally, though, Fisher set aside his straw hat and his religious qualms and stood up from his metal folding chair.

"In 1790, the first Amish moved to Leacock Township," he said. "Our people came here for the free country. They came to escape religious persecution.

"Now, if this keeps on, it looks as if we Amish will have to be driven out again from this garden spot. For what reason is it? The Amish will be driven out, not by persecution, but by prosperity. Because of prosperity, our children will be looking for another place."

Here in the heart of Lancaster County's Amish country, a proposal to turn 80 acres of rich farmland into a 100-home development called The Meadows has produced a collision of past and future. It has become the focus of a familiar battle between development and preservation, with a unique Pennsylvania Dutch twist. . . .

Amos Stoltzfus was born and raised on the farm he now wants to develop into $150,000 houses on the east edge of Intercourse. He turned 66 years old Tuesday, the same day he sat quietly in the township garage and listened to Fisher and other township residents criticize his plans.

He said nothing when his longtime next-door neighbors, Frank and June Hoover, begged the township supervisors to stop him from going ahead with the project.

"I've lived here all my life," said June Hoover, her voice cracking. "I've known Amos and his children a long, long time. I was always under the impression that your neighbor was more important than yourself, that if your neighbor was unhappy, you did what you could to please your neighbor.

"Amos," she said, turning to face Stoltzfus, seated two chairs away, "have you thought about our feelings? I still love you and want to be your friend, but have you thought about us? How would you and Mary feel if a big development went up behind you?"

Stoltzfus declined to say anything about his proposal, referring questions to his engineer and attorney.

But his son said the debate has been painful.

Myron Stoltzfus, 31, is chairman of the supervisors who next month will rule on the preliminary plan for Stoltzfus' development. The younger Stoltzfus has abstained from voting or participating in board discussion of his father's proposal, but that hasn't stilled complaints of preferential treatment from some opponents.

"It hurts, I have to admit it," said the younger Stoltzfus. "Dad has always been a good community man, a good neighbor and a great father. This cuts to the core."

But "where were these people [the project's opponents] when the developments they live in were built? Some of them are living in houses that are on land that 10 years ago I plowed myself. Now Dad wants to make it so someone else can experience the same thing they did, and he's accused of being greedy and selfish. Who's the ones really being selfish? They're not willing to share it with anyone else."

The township supervisors say that since Stoltzfus' farm was re-zoned several years ago—amid no public outcry—for residential use, there may be little they can do to stop the development when they vote July 10.

"If the [legal] conditions are met, we're not in a position to refuse it," said Frank Howe, vice chairman of the board.

"I'm for controlled growth, but I don't think it's fair to pick on one man," said Jake Smucker, another township supervisor. "The only way to not have growth is not to have any more babies, so what are you going to do?" . . .

"The hallmark of an advanced society is the care and regard it shows for those who can't speak for themselves," said Julie Lawson, who operates a gift shop in Intercourse. "And I think the Amish fall into that category."

"There is a place for development, but in Lancaster County, we have a unique situation. What works for everyone else doesn't nec-essarily work here."

◆

THE LAND OF GOD

(Reports from Intercourse, Pennsylvania, on a threat to the Amish
Community, by Peter Pringle, *London Sunday Independent*,
June 24, 1990)

The big surprise of the evening was when Gideon Fisher, an old
Amishman with a fine grey beard, got up to speak. No one had expected him to say anything because it is against the Amish religion
to be involved in controversy, and it is rare to hear an Amishman
pass judgment on anything—even the weather.

"I think," said Mr. Fisher reflectively, "that what has been said
here is rather interesting." There was a pause, as if that was all
he was going to say, and he nervously fingered the wide brim of
his straw hat. "You see," he continued, "two hundred years ago,
or more, our people came here to escape religious persecution in
Europe, and in those days the countryside was mostly woods. Well,
we helped to turn the land into what is now called the garden spot of
the world, but if this development keeps up it looks as if we're going
to be driven out again. This time it will not be religious persecution,
it will be the persecution of prosperity."

"Amen!" they cried.

And there was loud applause from the 150 local people who had
gathered last week on a humid summer evening in the garage of the
public works department to consider a proposal by Amos Stoltzfus,
an Amish farmer turned property developer, to transform part of his
fertile farmland into a new housing estate of nearly 100 homes. When
the clapping had died down, all eyes turned to the table where the
Board of Supervisors, the elected guardians of the community, sat
beside the American flag.

They had not applauded Mr. Fisher.

Quite the contrary: their faces were grim. They had made it clear
from the beginning of the meeting that they wanted Mr. Stoltzfus
to succeed in his application. "We're for controlled development,"
they said again and again. They produced consultants who held
handfuls of finely bound pale blue "studies" proclaiming that the
"development" was nothing but good for the township of Leacock.
The consultants said the extra 1,000 cars on the crowded little roads
each day would cause no problem to anyone, including the Amish

160

horse-drawn buggies, and that there would be no extra load on the local volunteer firemen, and no trouble with sewage lines.

In fact, said the Board with a unanimous, persuasive voice, progress of the kind Mr. Stoltzfus had in mind was exactly what the tiny communities of Lancaster County, like Leacock and Intercourse, Vintage and Paradise, Bird-in-Hand and Gap really needed.

The gathering in the garage could not have disagreed more. When someone suggested all those in favour of the project should stand, not a soul rose, not even Mr. Stoltzfus, who was beardless, and wore a smart blue jacket, tie, and grey trousers in contrast to the grubby tan shirts, black trousers, braces and waistcoats of the Amish farmers. He looked more like a developer from neighbouring New Jersey than a local man. He freely admitted he did not care what the community thought. Asked whether he would go ahead with his development even though the people seemed not to want it he replied, "Oh yes, very much so."

". . . I've got 74 acres up the road and it may be worth $2 million if I sell it for building lots," said an Amishman called Samuel who didn't want to give his other name. The thought of being forced off their land has emboldened more than one to speak out. "Perhaps," Samuel added with an unusual twinkle—unusual for the pale-faced, unsmiling Amish—"we should all take out a big advertisement in the *Wall Street Journal* saying, 'Amish Land For Sale,' and they would all come down from New York and New Jersey."

The behavior of the Board and Mr. Stoltzfus is neither outrageous nor new, although it was far from reassuring to the farmers. For several years now, the Amish farms have been steadily buried by bulldozers, and boxed in by industrial parks, shopping centres, and factory outlets. Five thousand new homes were started last year. . . .

The attitude of many local government officials is blatantly condescending. "We've bent over backwards to accommodate them," said Bob Alexander, a member of the Board of Supervisors. "I'm not here to run them out of town, but we have to have growth. What would happen if we didn't? Where would people live? I don't want to see them go. They're excellent farmers. I mean, I've got a lot of good Amish friends."

◆

The meeting concluded with the Supervisors announcing they would vote on the proposal July 10th. Many people milled around outside afterward as reporters interviewed Amish and non-Amish alike. Curiously, there was a feeling of great optimism in the gathering. Regardless of its final outcome, the meeting had blown everything wide open. As one Amishman said, "Cat's out of the bag now."

John Hostetler and Gideon Fisher walked slowly away from the township building, their heads leaning in toward one another as they talked quietly under the starry June night. Both men looked spent; even the reporters left them alone. I watched them drive away in John's car. It was well after nine P.M. Then the Armstrongs, Holmes Morton, Peter Pringle of the London newspaper, and I went to the White Horse Tavern along Route 340. We closed the place.

After the June 19th hearing, the Lancaster papers aired allegations by the Supervisors that "outsiders" were exploiting the Amish for their own land-preservation ends. Donna Clark went on the record assuring the press it was only outsiders who were still upset by "the Meadows." Jake Smucker was quoted as saying, "There's more outside opposition than inside, I know that for a fact. Those township citizens who voiced concern at the last meeting were pulled by outside people." *

And, once again, ugly, anti-Amish sentiment—in the forms of dismissal and denigration—appeared. Vice Chairman of the Supervisors Frank Howe said, "I don't see the concern from the bulk of the Amish over this particular subdivision."

But the most offensive remarks belonged to Donna Clark, who argued that if a no-growth land policy were instituted in Leacock Township, it would also mean prohibiting the Amish from building on their farmland. After pointing out that the Amish are "permitted" additions on their land for businesses and homes for Amish children when they marry, Clark said, "Are we going to stop giving them acres when Sadie gets married? We've bent over backward to accommodate the Amish." †

---

* Andrea Brown, untitled article from the *Lancaster New Era*, July 10, 1990, pages 1, 5.
† Brown, Ibid.

A few weeks later, back in Boston, I received the following letter from Paradise Township resident Elmer Fisher.

"As precincts chairman of the Pequea Valley Area," he began, "which encompasses Leacock, Paradise, Salisbury, and Sadsbury Townships, and Christiana Boro, I am writing this letter.

It seems rather strange that you, a resident of Boston, Massachusetts, should become involved in the affairs of Leacock Township. Suppose the residents of the Pequea Valley Area would meddle in the affairs of Boston, Massachusetts. Would you appreciate that? I doubt it.

Mr. Amos Stoltzfus, who owns The Meadows, is proceeding within the bounds of the local ordinances, the rules of the Lancaster County Planning Commission, the laws of Pennsylvania, and Federal regulations. He has a right to develope (sic) his land as he wishes. Why should you, who live hundreds of miles from Leacock Township, become involved in a matter such as this? It's none of your business.

We of Lancaster County, Pennsylvania, have been accustomed to solving our own problems. I see no need of your involvement in this situation. If we had need of help, we would very likely solicit it, but I'm sure we would not solicit the help of anyone from Boston, Massachusetts, nor Harvard University.

The Planning Commission of Leacock Township and the Board of Supervisors of this municipality are capable of making a final decision on The Meadows and do not need the interference from Randy Testa of Boston, Massachusetts.

I was glad for the opportunity to clarify for Fisher why I had in fact become so involved.

Equally as important, I wanted to make it clear to *myself* why I had been so involved. I spent several days working on a letter, and on July 22 I replied:

I appreciate your taking the time to write me a letter expressing your viewpoint. Let me answer the question you posed: "Why would you, who live hundreds of miles from Leacock Township, become involved in a matter such as this? It's none of your business."

For the past two years I have been living part of each month . . . among Amish friends of mine, assisting them with their business. When I first came to the County I had no intention of becoming involved in local politics, believe me. I should like to underscore that point. I came to . . . write my doctoral dissertation, period. So I guess I'm as surprised as you that I find myself involved in land disputes. Originally I was working merely to assist Professor John Hostetler in his work at Elizabethtown College.

But little by little I began to see that there was rampant evil afoot in Lancaster County in the guise of development and "progress." I became involved because I saw that many local people had become myopic to what was everywhere around them. You ought to have a sense of that, living as you do in a strip development of houses plopped in the middle of nowhere. If Lancaster County were just another farming county, one could well wonder what all the fuss was about. But it has a history of being one of the most productive farm counties in the United States—it is, as you know, the most productive nonirrigated farm county in America. This is quite a distinction. In addition, it is the home of the densest Amish population in the United States. Again, you ought to know that, given your last name and family heritage. I'm sure you are aware of a blatant disregard for the Amish way of life, particularly among developers, and among some "locals."

Amos Stoltzfus may be proceeding legally. Whether he is proceeding morally is altogether another question. From the time of the Pharisees we both well know that abiding by the letter of the law is no guarantee of membership in the Kingdom. Morality and legality often operate at odds with one another. So my involvement arises from a deep connection I have with my Amish friends . . . from my belief that Lancaster County is part of a national heritage and as such can afford my assistance, and from my conviction that "the Meadows" project is wrong.

Of course you see no need of my involvement. This is because your sympathies lie with Amos Stoltzfus. Luckily you and I live in a democracy—the essence of which is the tolerance of disagreement, the capacity to live with opposition, indeed to recognize it as necessary to a free society. This is not "interference" but the exercise of democracy. "The truth does not change according to our ability to stomach it emotionally."

The Planning Commission of Leacock Township is in collusion with Amos Stoltzfus. The word collusion means "an agreement between two or more people for a questionable purpose." This was apparent to anyone present at the June 19th Township hearing. I am within my rights to attend such meetings, to write letters to the editor about what I see, and to work through Harrisburg and at a national level to do what I think is morally/legally appropriate. I will continue to do so. More important, I am within my right to express my opinion and to work to see it come to fruition. And so are you. If you would restrict the opinions of others, you might want to visit the Soviet Union—a place where "interference" is no way tolerated.

If Amos Stoltzfus wanted to put a house of prostitution on his property, people would break down his door over the moral impropriety of such intention, even if he were to obtain the appropriate zoning (which given the local cast of characters, wouldn't be so hard to do!). But with housing, a clean/greed project, nobody objects. When one multiplies $150,000 by one hundred, it doesn't take a Harvard man to figure out there's a big take to be gotten. Well, in fact somebody does object—all the people surrounding the Stoltzfus property—local people—have petitioned and made their voices heard, without any help from me. Frank Howe himself said he'd never seen such a turnout for a township meeting. And if you were present, you'll recall that when those in favor of the project were asked to stand (by Dick Armstrong, a local man, for your information) no one stood. Not even Amos Stoltzfus or his sons present! But twice the rest of the room stood to express its opinion that the project is a bad idea. In my book democracy is based on the wishes of the majority. While Mr. Stoltzfus may be within his rights, the township supervisors are elected officials charged with enacting the wishes of the majority of township residents. This they will no doubt fail to do. Why? *This is my question to you.*

Finally, I would welcome involvement by residents of the Pequea Valley Area in Boston politics. It's a pretty corrupt city, and some of the township supervisors I've seen in action would feel right at home.

I hope this clarifies a notion or two for you. I appreciate the opportunity to clarify for you that I am not some random outsider. . . . My work has impelled me to act in Lancaster County, something I will continue to do. I would ask you, as a resident in a county with a deep religious heritage, to recall these words from Isaiah:

> *Woe to those who add house to house*
> *and join field to field*
> *until everything belongs to them*
> *and they are the sole inhabitants of the land. . . .*

I hope to meet you. . . . I'll bet you a cup of coffee and a doughnut "the Meadows" will be approved. What do you say?"

I did not attend the July 10th meeting—but over 150 township residents, English and Amish, and at least five television stations did.

So much for charges that "outsiders" were responsible for the size of the gathering. In fact, when asked by reporters if he was surprised by the turnout, Stoltzfus's lawyer, Donald LeFever, snarled, "No, I think you people have done a great job generating it." *

Camera crews surrounded the Board.

LeFever asked the Supervisors to consider the matter a month later, to allow Supervisors more time to consider engineering data

* Holland, W. Thompson, "Leacock Delays Vote on Development," *The Lancaster Intelligencer Journal*, July 11, 1990. page 1.

and other information pertinent to the project. The vote on "the Meadows" was delayed again, until August this time.

And that was that.

The gathering smelled a rat. "It's a scheme," one Amishman observed after the brief meeting. Another commented, "It's a smart game."*

"The Meadows" finally received preliminary approval in November 1990.

I said publicly I thought the Supervisors intentionally delayed their vote until Amish wedding season—the month of November—to approve the project, thereby ensuring that attention to the project among the Amish (and thus the media) would die down.

At the November meeting, local resident Sterling Schoen forced the Board to go on record with its connections to development-related industries. He stood up and asked all of the Supervisors about their business dealings. Jake Smucker said, "No comment." Donna Clark snapped, "It's a free market in this country."

Later they reluctantly disclosed the nature of their livelihoods: Donna Clark's family does electrical wiring in the housing industry, Jake Smucker installs roofing with his uncle's company, and Frank Howe is a supplier of building materials. Like many, I wonder whether Clark, Smucker, and Howe will reap the contractual benefits of "the Meadows." It wouldn't occur to such people to remove themselves from the bidding on "the Meadows." Donald LeFever has in fact pointed out that Pennsylvania's code of ethics doesn't view the potential for future contracting of awards as a conflict of interest. What is legal and what is moral are once again at odds in Leacock Township.

The Supervisors have recently facilitated the installation of a sewage system to accommodate "the Meadows" and Intercourse. Sewage lines are about to be extended into neighboring Gordonville, and there is talk that the nearby East Lampeter Township Police Department will soon be contracted to patrol Leacock Township, at a cost to township residents of an additional $300 per year in taxes. This tax hike will hit the Amish hard.

*Brown, Andrea, "Leacock Township Delays Vote on Housing Plan," *The Lancaster New Era*, July 11, 1990, page 1.

And as though this were not enough: in January 1992, Merle and Phyllis Good, proprietors of the "People's Place," an upscale tourist attraction in downtown Intercourse, unveiled plans with Lancaster-based developer Ed Drogaris to develop a thirty-five acre tract of farmland across the street from their operation. The farm had belonged to an Amishman who ran a business selling wooden furniture and lawn ornaments to tourists. It is rumored that Good, who is from a conservative Mennonite background, paid the farmer $2 million for the tract and is developing it to get out of heavy debt.

Good's proposed "village extension" includes plans for 75 to 125 houses, a village green, and shops. Because the "extension" was designed "with the character of the village in mind," it was cited as an example of "good" development and was initially backed by the Lancaster Farmland Trust, the American Farmland Trust, and the Historic Preservation Trust of Lancaster County. On further examination of the plans, however, the first two groups withdrew their support.

Michael Burnley of the Leacock Township sewer authority has expressed concern that the new development would require further expansion of the just-upgraded sewage system.

◆

As of this writing, it is rumored that ground for "the Meadows" will be broken in the spring of 1992. Amos Stoltzfus is silent about "when the bulldozers are coming."

PART NINETEEN

They have refreshed my spirit. You should recognize the
worth of such people. —1 Corinthians 16:18

◆

*August 1988. 7:30 P.M. Inside the Stoltzfus's barn, Levi, Katie, and I
are finishing up milking, telling jokes, laughing and talking. Suddenly Katie says, "My sisters were here the other day and Rebecca she
said to them, 'When Randy goes back to school, we'll have to bale the
hay by ourselves and go places with the horses.'" A silence falls.*

◆

En route to fetch Elam at the Lancaster Courthouse, where he and
two other Amish historians have been looking at documents, Rachel
and I are driving in a rental car. (I totaled the Horizon going through
an intersection in Lancaster at the end of July.) We drive together
often now. In fact, sometimes when we drive to her eldest daughter's
house, Rachel Senior rides in stocking feet.

Abruptly, she says, "I want to say a few things to you," and she
clears her throat. I look over. Rachel's eyes are shiny. I know what
is coming. This is about the end.

"You can always stay with us, for all that you've done. It doesn't
matter the time of day or night. You've got a place here. You know
we have a lot of outsiders stop by here asking questions, and you
know I don't say that to just anyone. But it doesn't matter, day or
night. You just get yourself here and you've always got a home."

Then after a pause Rachel says coyly, "Course, you can do a little for Elam. And me. Well, I'm *easy* to please. So that's what I wanted to tell you."

◆

Saturday, August 13, 1988. The last day of a summer in Paradise. I awaken at 6:30 A.M. Elam and Rachel are already up and around. I lie in bed for the next hour thinking about Levi and Katie milking in the barn, but I can't face the prospect of a last day of choring.

Rachel is ironing her white cap at the stove, warming a heavy, old-fashioned iron on a plate resting over one of the stove's gas burners.

Elam is at the kitchen table hunched over his stack of German prayer books. He is to preach at the funeral of a nine-year-old boy struck by a car. They will leave at eight o'clock.

We are all overtly lighthearted. But what is underneath comes through in moments. Elam, in his long black minister's coat, walks over to me and says abruptly, "Well, I want to thank you for all you done. I feel like you done more for us than we done for you."

"No, no, that's not true," I stammer, taking Elam's hand.

"Well, I have to hitch up the horses," he says and goes outside quickly, looking ministerial and somber and old as he puts on his black straw hat and gathers up his books. As he walks to the carriage I see that Elam wipes his eyes with a handkerchief.

Rachel and I are alone in the kitchen.

She quickly gathers up the breakfast dishes.

Turning from the sink, Rachel is in tears. "Thanks for every-thing," she says softly.

Instantly I am lost.

"Forgive me," she says through sobs, "for anything that wasn't—"

"—No, no . . . It was all good. . . ."

"You take care now and have a safe trip back."

"Godspeed," I whisper hoarsely.

We walk to the carriage in silence. Elam is already inside and Pat is shaking her reins from side to side, anxious to perk. Rachel steps up into the carriage and it leans hard to the left under her weight. The morning is hot and hazy under a bluish gray sky. A mother duck and eight ducklings rest along the banks of the creek. "See how the mother duck keeps track of her own," Rachel says distractedly. The wind chimes dangling from the porch are mournful.

And then there they are. Elam and Rachel, both in funereal black, seated in the carriage, Elam clutching Pat's reins.

"Giddyap," Elam says, and I watch the black carriage with the gray top turn and rumble down the Belmont Road.

Inside the house, on Elam and Rachel's side, Benuel sits on the enclosed porch. I give him my broken wind-up alarm clock and we play with it for a moment; the hands twirl around and around the clock face—first forward and then backward in a whir of gears, and Benuel is delighted. For me it is what has happened to notions of time, progress, and academic life in Cambridge. I wind the clock for Benuel again and he paddles off to show it to Rebecca.

I pack up my things and load up the rental car. Rachel has left me two shopping bags full of canned peaches, spreading cheese, some apples, and three jars of apricot jelly.

At eleven I am finished and join Katie and Levi on their side of the house. Benuel and Rebecca know I am leaving. They are quiet at the table. Katie has made a grand farewell meal: meatballs and, mashed potatoes and noodles and salad and applesauce and two hot shoo-fly pies direct from the oven, still bubbling. She offers me one to take along. But there is no room with all I will take with me (in the car or in my heart, which is about to break) and I hurry through the meal because if I look at Levi and Katie's children one more time I will have to unload the car and stay.

"Thank you for everything," I say to Katie, shaking her hand and holding it for a minute.

"Well! Thanks to *you*," she says. "Are you sure you won't take a pie along?"

"I wish I had room but I don't know what I'm going to do with what I have now when I get to the train station. But thank you."

Then I walk over to Levi and we shake hands.

"Thanks for being such a good teacher, Levi."

"Well, I try. I know there's a lot of things I could have explained better."

"No, no. It was all good. . . ."

We walk to the car. Again we shake hands in silence. Rebecca and Benuel stand on the porch with Katie. The baby is asleep. Again I say, "Thanks for teaching me all the things you taught me this summer."

"Well! With someone like you it was easy."

I get into the car and we shake hands again. In silence. I race out the field lane beeping the horn and take the back roads Elam showed me to Lancaster: out and around Intercourse, down Harvest Drive with stately Amish farms on either side of the road, then to Irishtown Road, to just past the farmer's market in Bird-in-Hand. The way Elam would go with a team: the Amish way.

I return the rental car in Lancaster and take a cab down Queen Street headed for the crumbly, grand Lancaster train station. My back sticks to my white shirt. I ask the cab driver to stop at a Turkey Hill Mini-Mart for a bottle of Gatorade. At the train station, I bring the shopping bags loaded with food, the two suitcases of clothing, and the Underwood typewriter up the steep marble steps to a long oak waiting bench. I keep looking at the sign above the clock that says LANCASTER with quotation marks around it, as if the sign were winking, until I fall sound asleep on the bench. I dream that the hands on the station clock are twirling and of horse hooves in starlight, and I nearly miss the eastbound train from Harrisburg to Philadelphia.

Aboard the train I rush to the club car, order three beers, guzzle them down, and look out the sooty train windows at fleeting Amish farmland—at all the farms that glide by between Lancaster and Parkesburg.

And then there is only embankment shrubbery and then the Lukens Steel Mills, vast and black and dead and rickety in Coatesville and then an endless strip of used-car dealerships and video rental stores and junk-food stands and then I am at the Paoli train platform, at my parents' house, back home but leaving home, yanked in the middle, twirling, the hands on the broken alarm clock, saying goodbye to a world which I have come to know as home.

◆

172

Goodbye to barefoot walks in the evening down the still-warm Belmont Road to the telephone shed while fireflies twinkle in the pasture and bullfrogs like twanging strings croak in Aaron Lapp's meadow.

Goodbye to the lantern etched with "home sweet home" left lit for me on the stove in the evenings.

Goodbye to Shorty sleeping on the kitchen table with his nose resting on an opened German Bible, sleeping Sunday mornings until Elam returns home from church.

Goodbye to the cows.

Goodbye to the blue mantel clock in Elam and Rachel's bedroom chiming Westminster style every fifteen minutes.

Goodbye to the white lace curtains and green shades billowing in my room from the breezes of traffic on the Belmont Road.

Goodbye to long, long talks with Rachel as she sits in her willow rocker crocheting just before bed, a colored thread coming out of a little hole carved in a plastic margarine bucket.

Goodbye to Elam hunched over his books at breakfast, lost in a story.

Goodbye to Katie, and Benuel and Rebecca and Samuel squirming at the breakfast table on Sunday mornings.

Goodbye to discussions of faith with Levi in the cow stables.

Goodbye.

Goodbye. Goodbye.

Godspeed.

Goodbye.

EPILOGUE

If my people, which are called by my name, shall humble themselves,

and pray, and seek my face, and turn from their wicked ways;

then will I hear from heaven, and will forgive

their sin, and will heal their land.

—II Chronicles 7:14.

◆

On the first day of choring in the barn for Levi, I was so excited to be feeding calves that I bounded over the wooden fence into the calf pen with all the assurance people like me are accustomed to displaying. A terrified bull calf kicked me so hard in the groin I rolled moaning on the ground for a long time.

But it was an important moment, a useful moment, a reminder of where I was and where I was not. In this new place, there was another way of living—and I had better learn it in a hurry.

On the last day of the summer, as the train roared back to my parents' house, I felt as if I had been kicked again. Back in Boston, nothing made sense. I took the subway each day to Revere Beach and sat for hours on its dreary ocean breakers trying to comprehend where I had been and how it related to academic life at Harvard. In the evenings I spent a lot of time drinking and writing at a bar near my home. I also spent a lot of time at St. Leonard's Catholic Church in the North End. I drank and wept and wrote. And I prayed.

Two weeks later I boarded AMTRAK's "Night Owl" and returned

to Lancaster County. I have been traveling back and forth monthly by train ever since. In many subsequent visits to the Stoltzfus farm I have finally begun to understand some things about who I am to the Stoltzfuses and to the Amish and who they are to me. These treks will continue. Without them, without the Stoltzfuses, life in Boston is unbearable.

◆

I first traveled to Pennsylvania and lived there for eighty-five consecutive days. I helped an Amish family so that I could write my dissertation about a moral community and get a doctorate in education. I journeyed as a teacher. I was not in a classroom or a lecture hall, a church or a monastery. I was in a home outside the village of Intercourse, and in a barn, in a cornfield, on a haywagon—all far from Harvard Square—in a rural area among people who cease their own formal schooling after the eighth grade. We were strangers to one another.

Little by little I came to know the Stoltzfuses and their world. I was taught how to catch a calf by tackling its front legs when it bolted from its pen; the trick to getting mules to back up; how to track the movement of thunderheads on a dark August afternoon; the way to know when corn is ready for harvest; and what it means to wake up each day before sunrise.

I began to see the outside world through the eyes of the Stoltzfus family. In moments I felt I had X-ray vision; at other times I thought I was blind. From the haywagon above the Belmont Road, I watched thousands and thousands of people—my people—pass by in campers and vans and tour buses. They were staring at the Stoltzfuses, staring at Levi driving his team, and they were staring at me. Maybe they thought I was Amish. After all, I had grown a thick beard, and there I was stacking bales on the haywagon. Their staring made me realize how thoroughly I am not Amish.

But among the Amish, I lost the sense of *who* I was. What had seemed vital in Cambridge seemed ridiculous in Paradise. I was driving the Horizon one day listening to "Pardon Me, You Left Your Tears on the Jukebox" playing on a country-western radio station out of Ephrata. Suddenly a newscaster cut in to report that President

Reagan was in the Soviet Union meeting with Mikhail Gorbachev. I turned off the radio until the music came back on. Only later did I realize the change I'd undergone. In Cambridge, I woke up faithfully every morning to coffee and National Public Radio news. In Lancaster County, news of the practical world sufficed.

◆

I would not want to become Amish. Nor could I. One could convert to Catholicism and still be a used-car dealer, an investment banker, or the owner of a beauty salon. These occupations do not exist within Amish society; it would be impossible to be an Amish novelist, professional hockey player, or Shakespearean actor. Being Amish is a faith and a completely encompassing way of life. For better and for worse, conversion to the Amish faith would mean leaving the worldly world behind. In part, it would require what Father Zossima in *The Brothers Karamazov* calls "a harsh and dreadful love."

Being Amish is not a "life-style." A life-style is something you can buy at a store and take out of a box, like styling gel or a food processor, and then discard when you have had enough. A life-style is marked by expendability and excess. A life-style is a series of marketed diversions. Faith, on the other hand, is not diversion. It is preoccupation.

Christians are told in the Letter to the Hebrews that faith is "confident assurance concerning what we hope for, and conviction about things we do not see." Flannery O'Connor wrote, "To find out about faith, you have to go among the people who have it and you have to go among the most sinless and intelligent ones if you're going to stand up intellectually to pagans and the general run of agnostics you're going to meet in the world."* You and I could argue about whether or not the Amish are really the most sinless. They know better than anyone that they are *not* saints. What is beyond dispute is their *struggle*—to remain a people of faith.

This struggle manifests itself in Lancaster County today through

* O'Connor, Flannery, *The Habit of Being: Letters of Flannery O'Connor*, selected and edited by Sally Fitzgerald (New York: Random House/Vintage Books, 1980), page 477.

economic tensions that gnaw away at the soul of the Amish community. The Amish live at a very different scale of economy than you or I in the outside world probably ever will because, as Wendell Berry has noted, in Amish society, the economy and the community are the same thing.* Berry reminds us that the word "economy" comes from the Greek word for "household" and that the Amish community is, in one sense, a large, extended family—one big household, if you will. By community mandate as designated by the particulars of their faith in God and thus their regard for one another, the Amish know freedom and personal restraint go together. The way they eat is the way they farm is the way they think is the way they behave with their neighbors. Life is an ongoing attempt to express "confident assurance" in the path to God they have chosen. Faith is the glue that joins these things, the blessed tie that binds.

Modernity is characterized by increments, by specialization, by parts, by refraction. Because there is little cohesion in the modern world, there is little faith in it. When people are isolated, divided within themselves and from others, faith and community are difficult, if not impossible. People require connection, neighbors in faith as well as in proximity, sustaining occupations, and a sense of continuity to help them stay whole and wholly occupied. These are the parameters of community and faith. Faith joins. Faith is connection. It "assures"—particularly in terrible times.

◆

Lately, I have been looking at how little and smooth my hands are. I realize I can type this page but I can't even fix my own toilet. My way of life presupposes that others will do for me what I myself do not want to do. Like George Orwell pondering coal and the backbreaking labor required to bring it up from the ground so that he could be comfortable enough in his study to write, I wonder about what I have become and about the invisible, innumerable human beings whose labor makes my scholarship possible.

Increasingly, I have grave doubts about academia and its central function, abstraction, particularly as I sit in the shadow of the

* Berry, Wendell, "Does Community Have a Value?" in *Home Economics* (Berkeley: North Point Press, 1987), page 189.

world's worldliest institution of higher learning. I begin to wonder if there is an inverse relationship between intellect and revelation.

In *The Imitation of Christ* it says, "At the Day of Judgement, we shall not be asked what we have read, but what we have done; not how eloquently we have spoken, but how holily we have lived."

If I have come to understand anything in Lancaster County it is that spirituality and practicality go hand in hand. Morality is a consequence of religion; it doesn't stand apart from it. This is Tolstoy's notion, not mine, but I have finally seen it in action—in people who don't generally read Tolstoy. Holiness, like morality, thrives in daily life.

Several years ago I was a section leader for a moral reasoning course offered in the Harvard Divinity School. We graded students on their capacity to construct reasoned, articulate, intellectual moral discourse. But I saw all too often that students could write with great eloquence and humanity about moral dilemmas, turn in their blue examination books, and then behave like skunks on the way out of the lecture hall. So could I.

Recently I have begun to ask some painful questions of my students—and myself: What will become of our parents in their old age? How will they be cared for? By whom? Have *we* considered caring for our parents in their infirmity? Otherwise, what will it mean to entrust their care to paid strangers?

Amish sons and daughters build apartments attached to the home farm for their parents. In separate quarters which are usually connected to the main house, Amish old people live out their lives near their children and grandchildren.* Work around the old folks' place is usually divided among the children. On a certain day of the week, one child comes to mow the lawn. On another day, another child

---

*This practice is now threatened in Lancaster County by recent changes in zoning ordinances designed to accommodate tract housing. In his article titled "When Do We Move?" in the April 1991 issue of an Amish monthly Abraham Blank wrote, "Due to the prosperity that has been brought to Lancaster County the farmers have a difficult problem to build an extension to a house for our elderly parents." The modern zoning laws have no exception to the restrictive clause, which, according to a zoning officer, does not create a problem because "the Rest Homes are built for the old folks, and it is not necessary to build extensions to farmhouses."

pulls up with a buggyful of granddaughters to wash and wax the floors.

Lest anyone idealize such a setup, the Amish, of course, are the first to tell you that having one's parents under the same roof in their twilight years can be extremely difficult. One friend calls it "a daily trial." But despite this, it is the way the Amish choose to care for their elderly.

In this and in many other hard choices that they are nonetheless willing to make, the Amish know that benefit and burden go hand in hand. They understand the relationship between these two conditions better than many of us in the outside world. They understand that the point of intersection between benefit and burden is where faith in God resides.

When, for example, students at Harvard tell me that Jesus's exhortation to "turn the other cheek" can't really be meant to be taken literally, I tell them in great detail about the Kings' buggy accident. Then I tell them that afterward, when the Kings learned of the sentencing of Marcial Chavez, the man whose van smashed through their lives, they did not seek retribution. Instead the Kings asked that he be shown every possible consideration under the law.

◆

Unless something is done to stop and *reverse* the trend, farmland in Lancaster County will continue to be blacktopped over. Many Old Order Amish doubt there is any real future left for them in Lancaster County, and the exodus has begun. The displacement of the Amish would remove the last obstacle to the total destruction of Lancaster County's remaining farmland by developers, officials of the Pennsylvania Dutch Visitors' Bureau, state legislators, farmers-turned-speculators, lawyers, the Lancaster Chamber of Commerce, the Pennsylvania Department of Transportation, advocates of "managed" growth, tourists, the Leacock Township Board of Supervisors, and an entire secular society obsessed with unchecked prosperity.

Yet no elected official seems capable of coming up with a solution to halt the destruction of Lancaster County and, thus, its Amish community. None is capable, or willing, politically; it would mean political suicide.

Here is an illustration of what I mean. Jerry Moll was appointed head of the Lancaster Chamber of Commerce. A thoughful, soft-spoken man recruited from Indiana, Moll was hired by the Chamber to tone down the Chamber's aggressively pro-development public image as epitomized by his predecessor, David Wauls.

Early in Moll's term, John Hostetler arranged for a quiet dinner between Jerry Moll and a group of Amish. After that experience, Moll began speaking publicly about "our Amish brethren," once even quoting Scripture to a group of civic leaders as they discussed economic growth: "Where there is no vision, the people perish."

Jerry Moll was fired early in his term and replaced by a Lancaster County native named Daniel Witmer—a failed farmer turned businessman.

To take on the formidable task of straightening out Lancaster County so that the Amish can thrive would take a moral leader, not just a politician. It would take someone with political tenacity fed by a wellspring of moral conscience and vision. It would take someone who recognized the unique contribution of the Plain Sect peoples; someone who realized that an important national, cultural, and moral presence is tilling the soil in its midst. Such vision does not exist in the Commonwealth of Pennsylvania. Left in the hands of politicians, the people may indeed perish. Or simply leave. On that day, I will pray, "Father, forgive us, for we knew exactly what we were doing."

◆

The Amish are not being shot for sport by soldiers, as the Sioux Indians were in another era. Nor are they being drowned or burned at the stake by public officials as their ancestors were in seventeenth-century Europe. In Lancaster County the Amish are being squeezed out one family at a time by a changing infrastructure mobilizing regulation, ordinance, money, and callousness disguised as concern for the economy.

Some Amish have chosen to squeeze themselves out of their own society, too, becoming ever more English, ever more worldly. I know of Amish businessmen with toll-free telephone numbers; I know of

Amishmen who keep outboard motor boats in their barns, who own the vans English drivers take them around the county in, Amish families who invite groups of tourists into their homes and cook up a storm for fifteen dollars a head. I can even take you to an Amish housing development in the making.

I once spoke to an irate Amishman who works on an English construction crew, right after the hearings in Leacock Township concerning the Stoltzfus farm. He said, "Why should our way of life concern you ?"

I turned to the man and said, "Because if your way of life falters, we all fall down. We need you to point out how far we have strayed."

◆

One night in Boston I sat at a bar with a friend who works as an Outward Bound instructor in Maine. We had been talking about what his students carry back into "the real world" from their intense experiences at sea. I told him about my summer in Lancaster County.

"And you?" he asked. "What will you carry back to your teaching from the Amish?" I have struggled to answer that question for over three years now. It makes me think about eggs.

At this writing, Grade B eggs—perfectly edible, farm-fresh white eggs—can be bought in Lancaster County (at the Esh Egg Farm in Gordonville, among other places) for about fifty cents a dozen. The owner of the egg farm lives on the premises and will probably come out to say hello. If he's not home, you pay for the eggs on the honor system: there's a Dutch Masters cigar box with money in it; you take what eggs you need and leave the money in the cigar box. Called "checks and dirties," the eggs need to be taken home and washed off before being eaten. They have caked, dried chicken manure on them and some are slightly cracked; otherwise the eggs are perfectly good. The Amish are regular patrons of the Esh Egg Farm.

When teaching, I sometimes ask my students to take this test. I say: the next time you go to the supermarket to buy eggs, lift open the egg carton, and if you find a dozen eggs in which one or two are cracked—or dirty—take *that* dozen to the checkout counter for purchase. Most students cannot do this. They become angry that I would even suggest such a thing. Which is exactly the point.

In the larger society, we think ourselves entitled to the best. We cannot stop to think that if we don't take the less-than-perfect dozen, one of two things will happen: either the eggs will stay on the shelf until they're rotten and thrown out, or someone else will have to buy them. We certainly won't take them. We are so accustomed to our "standard of living" (which comes at one another's expense) that such a choice becomes morally prohibitive. In tiny, daily moments we lose faith. As Dorothy Day said, we abdicate personal responsibility, repeating instead by our actions, the words of the first murderer: "Am *I* my brother's keeper?"

But on the day you and I can routinely go to the supermarket and buy the carton of cracked eggs—making a joyful noise unto the Lord as we do—the destruction of the Lancaster County Amish will come to a halt. Until then, the tiny whispering sound remains obscured.

The monk nodded. . . . "When one embraces the religious life and abandons the world one should go far away from one's home. It's not enough to change one's name if the water, the stones, the grass, the plants, the dust on the road are those of one's birthplace. One should go far away."

"I went far away," the priest confessed in a low voice. "But I couldn't stand it and I came back."

"Perhaps one should go to some place from which one can't come back."
—*Bread and Wine*,
Ignazio Silone

◆

AFTERWORD

BY ROBERT COLES

As I came to the end of Randy Testa's touching, compelling, wonderfully suggestive story of an Amish world in jeopardy, I remembered a conversation I had with the anthropologist Oscar Lewis, who was so skilled, subtle, energetic, and original-minded in his work as an observer of those who lived in worlds other than his own. We were talking about a study he was then contemplating, and I was interested in his "methodology." I had begun to use that word because I thought I should—evidence that I had an education, that I had a profession, that I was doing research, as opposed to mere listening and watching, followed by an attempt at the faithful, understandable presentation of what had been heard and seen and fathomed. I had thrown in a few other big-shot words and phrases as well, and expected a response in kind—no mere recital of what someone had in mind, his hopes and worries, his anticipations and hesitations, but, rather, a statement, an announcement, sprinkled liberally with formulations, concepts, even a theory or two which would give future readers plenty of pause. Instead I heard this brief comment: "At the end of all the exploration, an anthropologist will find himself—if he's lucky." A pithy remark, a modestly reflective comment, I recall thinking—spoken by someone who, in fact, had found out a lot, a whole lot, about many, many people other than Oscar Lewis. He had read my line of thinking—because his next words were addressed pointedly at me, and as I get ready to offer them to the reader I have in my mind an image of a man's face, his eyes looking directly at mine, his head tilted forward a bit, as if to give some physical substance to a thought being sent my way: "Maybe you'll discover that—learn that." Needless to say, those two verbs "discover" and "learn" can be used in quite another way—they become the asserted, privileged property of intellectuals who don't always manage to achieve the kind of modesty (maybe, too, the measure of grace) that had befallen one anthropologist rather late in his life.

This book, in its own thoughtful and unpretentious way, edges close, indeed, to the moral, if not spiritual terrain Professor Lewis was trying to convey, back then, for himself, for me, all too blinded at the time by ambitious exploratory visions, if not illusions, of my own. In a sense, this book, the author's first, has an instructively rare and impressive wisdom worthy of a much older and battle-worn investigator, who has, finally, with the help of countless others (called "subjects" or "instruments") come to his senses, and to a great truth: we help one another, hand one another along on this journey. For such an achievement alone, this book deserves our closest attention—a young observer's, a young pilgrim's singular discovery, granted him by a singular people, at once his fellow citizens, yet inhabitants of a world very much their own. But there are other, considerable virtues in the pages the reader has by now visited—a marvelous clarity of expression, a generous personal candor on the part of the narrator, whose gentle humor and mix of ironic bemusement and intense seriousness is both notable and rare. To expand upon the farewell of sorts Oscar Lewis graciously extended to me a quarter of a century ago (he died, alas, only a short while after that conference we both attended had been convened): to attend closely the voices of others is to explore, gradually, both the pitch of one's own voice and the message it wants to convey. For this book's author, the voice is not only one of wry wistfulness, or at moments, regret, even outrage, but also one of passionate concern, of open affection. Yes, he has told us that the Amish are, finally, our fellow human beings, warts and all. But they are, too, a people of considerable moral energy, and of no small amount of courage—a willingness to stand on their very own feet, no matter the burdens and costs. If they are to go, if they are to surrender to a larger culture, with all its powers of persuasion, seduction, even intimidation, then the loss will surely not be only theirs, as this book constantly reminds us.

Those of us fortunate enough to have met Randy Testa on the preceding pages have, really, been the recipients of a gift—a moral witness has shared his experiences with us, and thereby helped us stop for a while, in order to look inward, perhaps see ourselves through a lens that is at once Amish (that is, profoundly spiritual) and yet, too, that of late twentieth-century secular America: the tightrope Randy Testa walks, even as his friends in Lancaster County, Pennsylvania, do, and one suspects, many of us, also, who have joined them as a consequence of our encounter with this extraordinarily telling book.

UNIVERSITY PRESS OF NEW ENGLAND publishes books under its own imprint and is the publisher for Brandeis University Press, Brown University Press, University of Connecticut, Dartmouth College, Middlebury College Press, University of New Hampshire, University of Rhode Island, Tufts University, University of Vermont, and Wesleyan University Press.

When he is not in Lancaster County, Randy-Michael Testa is a teacher, writer, and editor in Cambridge, Massachusetts.

Susie Riehl lives with her husband and six children on a small farm near the town of White Horse, in Lancaster County, Pennsylvania. With the support of her family, since 1987 she has made public her artwork depicting the life of her people, the Old Order Amish.

Library of Congress Cataloging-in-Publication Data
Testa, Randy-Michael.
    After the fire : the destruction of the Lancaster County Amish / Randy-Michael Testa ; foreword by John A. Hostetler ; afterword by Robert Coles ; illustrations by Susie Riehl.
    p.   cm.
    ISBN 0–87451–587–4
    1. Amish—Pennsylvania—Lancaster County.   2. Lancaster County (Pa.)—Social conditions.   I. Title.
    F157. L2 T47   1992
    974.8′150088257—dc20   92–11529

⊗